Multicultural Education for Educational Leaders

Critical Black Pedagogy in Education
Series Editor: Abul Pitre

Titles in the Series

Educating African American Students: Foundation, Curriculum, and Experiences, edited by Abul Pitre, Esrom Pitre, Ruth Ray, and Twana Hilton-Pitre (2009)

African American Women Educators: A Critical Examination of Their Pedagogies, Education Ideas, and Activism from the Nineteenth to the Mid-twentieth Century, edited by Karen A. Johnson, Abul Pitre, and Kenneth L. Johnson (2013)

Multicultural Education for Educational Leaders

Critical Race Theory and Antiracist Perspectives

Abul Pitre, Tawannah G. Allen, and Esrom Pitre

ROWMAN & LITTLEFIELD
Lanham • Boulder • New York • London

Published by Rowman & Littlefield
A wholly owned subsidary of The Rowman & Littlefield Publishing Group, Inc.
4501 Forbes Boulevard, Suite 200, Lanham, Maryland 20706
www.rowman.com

Unit A, Whitacre Mews, 26-34 Stannary Street, London SE11 4AB

British Library Cataloguing in Publication Information Available

Library of Congress Cataloging-in-Publication Data

Library of Congress Cataloging-in-Publication Data Available
ISBN 978-1-4758-1400-2 (cloth : alk. paper) -- ISBN 978-1-4758-1401-9 (pbk. : alk. paper) -- ISBN
978-1-4758-1402-6 (electronic)

Contents

Contents

Foreword

KNOWING THE TRUTH: THE CHALLENGE FOR EDUCATIONAL
LEADERSHIP

"And you will know the truth, and the truth will make you free." – John 8:32

The truth in American society with regard to diversity and race relations remains elusive. As I write this foreword, protesters are marching in Ferguson, MO because of the shooting death of an unarmed African American teenager by a White police officer. This death comes on the heels of another, in New York City, of an African American male who was placed in a choke hold by a police officer. Unfortunately, these kinds of deaths are not new or shocking; among others, memories of Trayvon Martin, an unarmed African American high-school student shot to death by a neighborhood watch coordinator, still resonate.

The truth is that far too many African Americans have horror stories about their interactions with the police. Too often African Americans are stereotypically viewed as criminals, suspects, troublemakers, drug dealers, and any number of other things. But the problem doesn't stop there. If American law enforcement on the street can act on preconceived notions about people of color, how can America's public schools be safe for American children of color?

The United States of today is an obviously racially and ethnically diverse nation. Demographic projections indicate that by 2040, Hispanic, African American, and Asian populations will increase to the point that Whites will comprise 50.1% of the total population (Brooks, 2012). This shift will have profound implications for K-12 education. Currently, most of the country's increasingly diverse student population is being taught and led by teachers and administrators who are predominantly White (Tillman, 2003). This is not to imply that we must exclusively have educators of color working with students of color. "More important is the attitude and expectations of teachers and school leaders" (McCray & Beachum, 2014, p. 92).

In the United States, the truth is that most Americans have been born into homogeneous communities (majority White, majority African American, majority Hispanic, etc.). As we mature, we are molded and shaped by our experiences in our particular community (Harro, 2000); we absorb and internalize its values, beliefs, stereotypes, and practices (Tatum, 1997; 2007). Although many educators claim that they are neutral and unbiased, all human beings have biases: complete neutrality is extremely difficult if not impossible. To complicate matters, the overarching message that gets repeated situates people of color as inferior to Whites (Zamudio, Russell, Rios, & Bridgeman, 2011). In schools, this attitude seems to lead to overaggressive discipline applied to students of color, lowered expectations of these students, and/or a deficit perspective overall. Villegas and Lucas (2002) wrote:

> Teachers [and school leaders] looking through the deficit lens believe that the dominant culture is inherently superior to the cultures of marginalized groups in society. Within this framework, such perceived superiority makes the cultural norms of the dominant group the legitimate standard for the United States and its institutions. Cultures that are different from the dominant norm are believed to be inferior... Such perceptions inevitably lead teachers to emphasize what students who are poor and of color cannot do rather than what they already do well. (p. 37)

Such perceptions are particularly problematic for fields such as educational leadership, which has traditionally not utilized or valued critical frames of analysis.

Educational leadership largely deals with school administration, direction, and/or management. It has largely been informed by business, management approaches, and organizational behavior/theory (English, 2008; McCray & Beachum, 2014). Dantley (2002) indicated that educational leadership has "borrowed idioms and syntax from economics and the business world all in an effort to legitimate itself as a valid field" (p. 94). Although there are some obvious lessons to be learned from fields such as business, economics, and organizational behavior, the way these fields presents material that can be applied to education naturally positions the school leader as authoritarian yet also neutral, apolitical, and/or unresponsive about issues of race. Villegas and Lucas (2002) asserted that this duality causes educators to be technicians more than agents of change.

This orientation has left teachers and administrators unprepared for school realities in the twenty-first century. As student diversity increases, so does the need to connect to many types of communities and the need to expand the traditional school mission to treat students from all communities as equally valuable within the educational process. New, inclusive frameworks are needed to help school leaders clarify and make meaning of complex social situations.

Critical race theory (CRT), an academic discipline that examines society and culture at the juncture of race, law, and power, can be a useful and insightful tool for educational leadership. CRT is "a framework that attempts to provide unique ways to examine, analyze, and explain the roles, rules, and recognition of race and racism in society. It has its origins in law as a response to critical legal studies (CLS). Critical race theory views racism as a natural aspect of everyday life in the United States, thus permeating everything from academic disciplines to legal decisions to the modern workplace" (Beachum, 2012, p. 907). Some of the major ideas and tenets of CRT include:

1. Racism as a permanent aspect of American life.
2. Skepticism toward claims of "neutrality, objectivity, colorblindness, and meritocracy."
3. The necessity of challenging ahistorical analyses and supporting contextual/historical ones.
4. Recognition of the importance of the voices and stories of people of color.
5. Emphasis on interdisciplinary approaches.
6. Dismantling of racial oppression as well as the elimination of oppression in all forms. (Matsuda, Lawrence, Delgado, & Crenshaw, 1993, p. 6)

Many Americans are disheartened by the idea of racism being a permanent aspect of our national life. Some even reject it outright. But if we examine it more closely, we see that it is very real and relevant. People of color in K-12 schools (from students to teachers and administrators) may encounter microaggressions on a daily basis. These are negative racial interactions that result in the insulting, defamation, or disrespectful treatment of people of color (Tatum, 1997). The permanence of racism also explains how the contributions, intellects, histories, and cultures of students of color are systematically devalued (Kailin, 2002). Perry (2003) provided a powerful explanation:

> Today, the ideology of Black intellectual inferiority is expressed in the media, which inserts itself into all aspects of our lives. The ideology of African American inferiority is perhaps more robust today, in terms of its impact on students, than it was in the pre-Civil Rights era... After all, we live in the post-Civil Rights era. The society is now open. Few respectable people will publicly assert that Black people are intellectually inferior. The visible, in-your-face manifestations of oppression have been mostly eliminated. But you can scarce-

ly find a Black student who cannot recall or give you a litany of instances
when he or she was automatically assumed to be intellectually incompetent.
(p. 97)

Another pillar of CRT is counter-storytelling or counternarratives, meaning
that people of color must be able to present their own recitations, positions,
and experiences and have those presentations taken seriously—as lived experience that is in itself a legitimate form of knowledge. A large part of how we
learn is dictated by who controls the master narratives that make up the
commonly accepted preponderance of ideas, thoughts, and experiences that
we call "knowledge." If the people who control not only the dissemination
but the very content of knowledge have grown up in homogeneous social
worlds, and if their views of humanity have been shaped by constant messages of White supremacy and the inferiority of non-Whites, then we should
expect that their interpretations of information that contradicts their knowledge and experience will be biased toward Whiteness. In particular, we
should expect that they will (whether subtly or consciously) subvert, soften,
or even deny the impact of issues having to do with race.

According to DeCuir and Dixon (2004) "The use of counterstories allows
for the challenging of privileged discourses, the discourses of the majority,
therefore, serving as a means for giving voice to marginalized groups" (p.
27). Counter-stories and counternarratives thus allow for different perspectives and also build community cohesion as others connect to the messages
they convey (Delgado, 1989). In schools, the embrace of counternarratives
could mean that teachers and school leaders create more opportunities for
student voices, especially for students of color.

This book, *Multicultural Education for Educational Leaders: Critical
Race Theory and Antiracist Perspectives* is of immediate value. It is timely,
because school leaders need tools for investigation, introspection, interroga-
tion, and information. For their part, educational researchers need information about how critical race theory can be conceived and applied in school
settings. Within these covers they will find thoughtful consideration of a
broad range of topics related to CRT and antiracist perspectives. This work
represents a significant contribution to the understanding of how race, inequality, and privilege impact education.

Sometimes knowing the truth is not easy. This book presents topics that
are complex, and that will be uncomfortable for many readers—sometimes
profoundly so. But in order for significant change to occur, we must be made
to feel uncomfortable at times. Gorski (2006) explained that part of the
reason multicultural education has not become the norm in America is because Americans value comfort, more than we value change. I hope that this
book informs, enlightens, and causes you, the reader, enough discomfort to
participate in making changes for all of our students.

REFERENCES

Beachum, F. D. (2012). Critical Race Theory and educational leadership. In F. W. English (Ed.), *The handbook of educational theories* (pp. 907–912). Charlotte, NC: Information Age.

Brooks, J. S. (2012). *Black school, White school: Racism and educational (mis)leadership.* New York: Teachers College Press.

Dantley, M. E. (2002). Uprooting and replacing positivism, the melting pot, multiculturalism, and other impotent notions in educational leadership through an African American perspective. *Education and Urban Society, 34*(3), 334–352.

DeCuir, J. T., & Dixson, A. D. (2004). "So when it comes out, they aren't that surprised that it is there": Using critical race theory as a tool of analysis of race and racism in education. *Educational Researcher, 33*(5), 26–31.

Delgado, R. (1989). Storytelling for oppositionist and others: A plea for narrative. *Michigan Law Review, 87*(8), 2411–2441.

English, F. W. (2008). *The art of educational leadership: Balancing performance and accountability.* Thousand Oaks, CA: Sage Publications.

Gorski, P. (2006). The unintentional undermining of multicultural education: Educators at the crossroads. In J. L. Landsman and C. W. Lewis (Eds.), *White teachers/diverse classrooms: A guide to building inclusive schools, promoting high expectations, and eliminating racism* (pp. 61–78). Sterling, VA: Stylus.

Harro B. (2000). The cycle of socialization. In M. Adams, W. J. Blumenfield, R. Castaneda, H. W. Hackman, M. L. Peters, and X. Zuniga (Eds.), *Reading for diversity and social justice: An anthology on racism, anti-Semitism, sexism, heterosexism, ableism, and classism* (pp. 79–82). New York: Routledge.

Kailin, J. (2002). *Antiracist education: From theory to practice.* New York: Rowan & Littlefield.

Matsuda, M., Lawrence, C., Delgado, R., & Crenshaw, K. (Eds.) (1993). *Words that wound: Critical race theory, assaultive speech and the first amendment.* Boulder, CO: Westview.

McCray, C. R., & Beachum, F. D. (2014). *School leadership in a diverse society: Helping schools prepare all students for success.* Charlotte, NC: Information Age.

Perry, T. (2003). Up from the parched earth: Toward a theory of African-American achievement. In T. Perry, C. Steel, and A. G. Hilliard (Eds.), *Young, gifted and Black: Promoting high achievement among African-American students* (pp. 1–108). Boston: Beacon.

Tatum, B. D. 1997. *Why are all the Black kids sitting together in the cafeteria? and other conversations about race.* New York: Basic.

————— 2007. *Can we talk about race? and other conversations in an era of school resegregation.* Boston, MA: Beacon.

Villegas, A. M., & Lucas, T. (2002). *Educating culturally responsive teachers: A coherent approach.* Albany, NY: State University of New York Press.

Zamudio, M. M., Russell, C., Rios, F. A., & Bridgeman, J. L. (2011). *Critical race theory matters: Education and ideology.* New York: Routledge.

Series Foreword

Historically, the state of Black education has been at the center of American life. When the first Blacks arrived to the Americas to be made slaves, a process of *mis-education* was systematized into the very fabric of American life. Newly arrived Blacks were dehumanized and forced through a process that has been described by a conspicuous slave owner named Willie Lynch as a "breaking process": "Hence the horse and the nigger must be broken; that is, break them from one form of mental life to another—keep the body and take the mind" (Hassan-EL, 2007, p. 14). This horrendous process of breaking the African from one form of mental life into another included an elaborate educational system that was designed to kill the creative Black mind.

Elijah Muhammad called this a process that made Black people blind, deaf, and dumb—meaning the minds of Black people were taken from them. He proclaimed, "Back when our fathers were brought here and put into slavery 400 years ago, 300 [of] which they served as servitude slaves, they taught our people everything against themselves" (Pitre, 2008, p. 6). Woodson (2008) similarly decried, "Even schools for Negroes, then, are places where they must be convinced of their inferiority. The thought of inferiority of the Negro is drilled into him in almost every class he enters and almost in every book he studies" (p. 2).

Today, Black education seems to be at a crossroads. With the passing of the No Child Left Behind Act of 2001, schools that serve a large majority of Black children have been under the scrutiny of politicians who vigilantly proclaim the need to improve schools while not realizing that these schools were never intended to educate or educe the divine powers within Black people. Watkins (2001) posits that after the Civil War, schools for Black people— particularly those in the South—were designed by wealthy philanthropists. These philanthropists designed "seventy-five years of education for blacks" (pp. 41–42). Seventy-five years from 1865 brings us to 1940, and today we are still being impacted by seventy-five years of scripted education; to truly understand the plight of Black education, one has to consider the historical impact of seventy-five years of scripted education and its influence on the present state of Black education.

Presently, schools are still controlled by ruling-class Whites who hold major power. Woodson (2008) saw this as a problem in his day and argued, "The education of the Negroes, then, the most important thing in the uplift of Negroes, is almost entirely in the hands of those who have enslaved them and now segregate them" (p. 22). Here, Woodson cogently argues for historical understanding: "To point out merely the defects as they appear today will be of little benefit to the present and future generations. These things must be viewed in their historic setting. The conditions of today have been deter-mined by what has taken place in the past" (p. 9). Watkins (2001) sum-marizes that the "white architects of black education . . . carefully selected and sponsored knowledge, which contributed to obedience, subservience, and political docility" (p. 40). Historical knowledge is essential to under-standing the plight of Black education.

A major historical point in Black education was the famous *Brown v. Board of Education of Topeka, Kansas*, in which the Supreme Court ruled that segregation deprived Blacks of educational equality. Thus, schools were ordered to integrate with all deliberate speed. This historic ruling has contin-ued to impact the education of Black children in myriad and complex ways.

To date, the landmark case of *Brown v. Board of Education* has not lived up to the paper that it was printed on. Schools are more segregated today than they were at the time of the *Brown* decision. Even more disheartening is that schools that are supposedly desegregated may have tracking programs such as "gifted and talented" that attract White students and give schools the appearance of being integrated while actually creating segregation within the school. Spring (2006) calls this "second-generation segregation" and asserts: "Unlike segregation that existed by state laws in the South before the 1954 *Brown* decision, second generation forms of segregation can occur in schools with balanced racial populations; for instance, all White students may be placed in one academic track and all African American or Hispanic students in another track" (p. 82). In this type of setting, White supremacy may become rooted in the subconscious minds of both Black and White students. Nieto and Bode (2012) highlight the internalized damage that tracking may have on students when they say students "may begin to believe that their placement in these groups is natural and a true reflection of whether they are 'smart,' 'average,' or 'dumb'" (p. 111).

According to Oakes and Lipton (2007), "African American and Latino students are assigned to low-track classes more often than White (and Asian) students, leading to two separate schools in one building—one [W]hite and one minority" (p. 308). Nieto and Bode (2012) argue that the teaching strategy in segregated settings "leaves its mark on pedagogy as well. Students in the lowest levels are most likely to be subjected to rote memorization and static teaching methods" (p. 111). These findings are consistent with Lipman's (1998): "Scholars have argued that desegregation policy has been framed by what is in the interest of [W]hites, has abstracted from excellence in education, and has been constructed as racial integration, thus avoiding the central problem of institutional racism" (p. 11). Hammond-Darling (2005) is not alone, then, in observing that "the school experiences of African American and other minority students in the United States continue to be substantially separate and unequal" (p. 202).

Clearly, the education of Black students must be addressed with a sense of urgency like never before. Lipman (1998) alludes to the crisis of Black education, noting that "the overwhelming failure of schools to develop the talents and potentials of students of color is a national crisis" (p. 2). In just about every negative category in education, Black children are overrepresented. Again Lipman (1998) alludes, "The character and depth of the crisis are only dimly depicted by low achievement scores and high rates of school failure and dropping out" (p. 2).

Under the guise of raising student achievement, the No Child Left Behind Act has instead contributed to the demise of educational equality for Black students. Hammond-Darling (2004) cites the negative impact of the law: "The Harvard Civil Rights Project, along with other advocacy groups, has warned that the law threatens to increase the growing dropout rate and push-out rates for students of color, ultimately reducing access to education for these students rather than enhancing it" (p. 4). Asante (2005) summarizes the situation thus: "I cannot honestly say that I have ever found a school in the United States run by whites that adequately prepares black children to enter the world as sane human beings . . . an exploitative, capitalist system that enshrines plantation owners as saints and national heroes cannot possibly create sane black children" (p. 65). The education of Black students and its surrounding issues indeed makes for a national crisis that must be put at the forefront of the African American agenda for liberation.

In this series, *Critical Black Pedagogy in Education*, I call upon a wide range of scholars, educators, and activists to speak to the issues of educating Black students. The series is designed to not only highlight issues that may negatively impact the education of Black students but also to provide possibilities for improving the quality of education for Black students. Another major goal of the series is to help preservice teachers, practicing teachers, administrators, school board members, and those concerned with the plight of Black education by providing a wide range of scholarly research that is thought provoking and stimulating. The series will cover every imaginable aspect of Black education from K–12 schools to higher education. It is hoped that this series will generate deep reflection and catalyze action—praxis to uproot the social injustices that exist in schools serving large numbers of Black students.

In the past, significant scholarly research has been conducted on the education of Black students; however, there does not seem to be a coherent theoretical approach to addressing Black education that is outside of European dominance. Thus, the series will serve as a foundation for such an approach—an examination of Black leaders, scholars, activists, and their exegeses and challenge of power relations in Black education. The idea is based on the educational philosophies of Elijah Muhammad, Carter G. Woodson, and others whose leadership and ideas could transform schools for Black students. One can only imagine how schools would look if Elijah Muhammad, Carter G. Woodson, Marcus Garvey, or other significant Black leaders were in charge. Additionally, the election of Barack Hussein Obama as the first Black president of the United States of America offers us a compelling examination of transformative leadership that could be inculcated into America's schools. The newly elected president's history of working for social justice, his campaign theme of "Change We Can Believe In," and his inaugural address that challenged America to embrace a new era are similar to the ideas embodied in *Critical Black Pedagogy in Education*.

This series is a call to develop an entirely new educational system. This new system must envision how Black leaders would transform schools within the context of our society's diversity. With this in mind, we are looking not only at historical Black leaders but also at contemporary extensions of these great leaders. Karen Johnson (2014) describes the necessity for this perspective: "There is a need for researchers, educators, policy makers, etc. to comprehend the emancipatory teaching practices that African American teachers employed that in turn contributed to academic success of Black students as well as offered a vision for a more just society" (p. 99). Freire (2000) also lays a foundation for critical Black pedagogy in education by declaring, "it would be a contradiction in terms if the oppressors not only defended but actually implemented a liberating education" (p. 54). Thus, critical Black pedagogy in education is a historical and contemporary examination of Black leaders (scholars, ministers, educators, politicians, etc.) who challenged the European dominance of Black education and suggested ideas for the education of Black people.

Multicultural Education for Educational Leaders: Critical Race Theory and Antiracist Perspectives is a compelling book that contains reflective chapters written by educational leaders regarding the importance of multicultural education. The contributors engage in candid conversations about critical multicultural education, particularly discussing issues related to race and racism. Moving away from the additive and feel-good approaches to multicultural education, the chapters in this book present a critical approach to understanding multicultural education, providing new insights for preservice and in-service educational leaders. Additionally, critical theories of education are discussed, which include topics such as *critical race theory*, *critical White studies*, *critical Black pedagogy in education*, and *antiracist education* covered from the perspective of educational leaders.

The book is a good resource for educational leaders looking for critical insights regarding personal transformation and school transformation. Emerging from this collection of chapters is an approach to multicultural education that provides educational leaders with a moral and spiritual compass that could radically change the perspectives of educational leaders and the programs that prepare them. It is a readable book that challenges educational leaders to think about multicultural education in educational settings.

The book is a welcome addition to the literature on Black education. Similar to Joyce King's (2005) *Black Education: A Transformative Research and Action Agenda for the New Century*, this book addresses research issues raised in the Commission on Research in Black Education (CORIBE). Like CORIBE's agenda, this book focuses on "using culture as an asset in the design of learning environments that are applicable to students' lives and that lead students toward more analytical and critical learning" (p. 353). The book is indeed provocative, compelling, and rich with information that will propel those concerned with equity, justice, and equality of education into a renewed activism.

Abul Pitre
Series Editor

REFERENCES

Asante, K. (2005). *Race, rhetoric, & identity: The architecton of soul*. Amherst, NY: Humanity Books.

Freire, P. (2000). *Pedagogy of the oppressed*. New York: Continuum.

Hammond-Darling, L. (2004). From "separate but equal" to "no child left behind": The collision of new standards and old inequalities. In D. Meier & G. Wood (Eds.), *Many children left behind: How the No Child Left Behind Act is damaging our children and our schools* (pp. 3–32). Boston: Beacon Press.

Hammond-Darling, L. (2005). New standards and old inequalities: School reform and the education of African American students. In J. King (Ed.), *Black education: A transformative research and action agenda for the new century* (pp. 197–224). Mahwah, NJ: Lawrence Erlbaum Associates.

Hassan-EL, K. (2007). *The Willie Lynch letter and the making of slaves*. Besenville, IL: Lushena Books.

Johnson, K., & A. Pitre (Eds.). (2014). *African American women educators: A critical examination of their pedagogies, educational ideas, and activism from the nineteenth to the midtwentieth centuries*. Lanham, MD: Rowman and Littlefield Education.

King, J. E. (Ed). (2005). *Black education: A transformative research and action agenda for the new century*. Mahwah, NJ: Lawrence Erlbaum Associates.

Lipman, P. (1998). *Race, Class, and Power in School Restructuring.* Albany, NY: SUNY Press.

Nieto, S., & P. Bode. (2012). *Affirming diversity: The sociopolitical context of multicultural education* (6th ed.). Boston: Allyn and Bacon.

Oakes, J., & M. Lipton. (2007). *Teaching to change the world* (3rd ed.). Boston: McGraw-Hill.

Pitre, A. (2008). *The education philosophy of Elijah Muhammad: Education for a new world* (2nd ed.). Lanham, MD: University Press of America.

Spring, J. (2006). *American education.* New York: McGraw-Hill.

Watkins, W. (2001). *The White architects of Black education: Ideology and power in America, 1865–1954.* New York: Teachers College Press.

Woodson, C. G. (2008). *The mis-education of the Negro.* Drewryville, VA: Kha Books.

Preface

Educational leaders are bombarded on a daily basis with a plethora of issues from diverse constituents. In the highly politicized educational arena, test scores and prepackaged curricula have become the order of the day. In their attempt to satisfy politicians' needs and mandates that come from on high, educational leaders are faced with a moral and ethical dilemma of how to best serve the needs of their students.

Of particular concern are those schools that have high concentrations of low-income, non-White-majority student populations where testing data reveals an achievement gap between Black and Latino students as compared to their White peers. Paige and Witty (2010), in their book, *The Black-White Achievement Gap: Why Closing It Is the Greatest Civil Rights Issue of Our Time*, stress the need for Black leaders to become more involved in what they see as the new civil rights issue in America. However, while Paige and Witty may be on point in declaring that the Black and White achievement gap is a crisis, the burden of transforming schools does not rest solely on the shoulders of Black leadership—we need transformative educational leaders who envision new ways of schooling and education.

Transformative suggests that school leaders need to undergo a transformation in terms of how they see the role of schools in the education process. Shields (2011) succinctly captures the meaning of transformative writing: "To be truly transformative, the process of leadership must be linked to the ends of equity, inclusion, and social justice" (p. 5). Essential to developing transformative educational leaders are theoretical concepts found in critical multicultural education. In this book we present a critical multicultural education perspective that is rooted in examining racism in schools. While the language of the book is written to inflame educational leaders and those who prepare them, we are hopeful that those who read the text will be able to bear our critiques of the inequitable schooling conditions that exist in too many public schools.

In using the term *inflame*, what is suggested is that the old ideas of thinking about leading in public schools will be set ablaze, giving rise to a new way of leading, teaching, and educating. While this book is heavily focused on critical race theory and antiracist concepts with a particular focus on White educators, we are in no way trying to place the blame entirely on the shoulders of White educators. In fact, when speaking about White educators we are particularly addressing a mind-set that Whiteness does not necessarily embody a skin color. Carter G. Woodson perhaps had such in mind when he declared that a Black teacher was in many cases a White teacher, meaning that the thinking of Black teachers aligned with White supremacist ideology. Freire (2000) called this an *internalization process*, whereby the oppressed internalize the image of their oppressors and ultimately imitate them. Thus, it is imperative that you read the book as a critical presentation of concepts designed to help educational leaders reflect, act, and eradicate racism in schools.

As a group of scholars living in the South where Black students are the majority population in some regions and schools, we focus on Black education. Additionally, one chapter argues that educational leaders need more knowledge on transformative Black leadership. What emerges from this is a concept called *critical Black pedagogy in education*, which has been outlined in the series foreword. The ideas embodied in critical Black pedagogy in education are *Afrocentric education, multicultural education, critical pedagogy*, and *African American spirituality.*

The concepts presented in the book will perhaps be new to a majority of educational leaders who have been trained in school administration programs that do not address the cultural aspects of leadership but focus more heavily on a scientific management approach to school leadership. Concepts such as racism, critical pedagogy, antiracist education, and social justice may be shocking for some educational leaders, and this should not be alarming.

Some contributors to this book experienced an initial shock, as we had never considered analyzing school and education from this framework. Over the course of time as we engaged critical readings and held intense conversations, the scales were removed from our eyes, allowing us to become new. This newness of thought has created a process that confirms that human beings are incomplete. We are constantly becoming and unbecoming!

Contributors to this volume cogently express the concept of becoming and unbecoming. We are becoming more aware of the sociopolitical aspects of schooling and education that create certain kinds of antieducation environments and behaviors. This has helped us to move from the *cultural deprivation theory* to look more inwardly at ourselves and the role we play as educational leaders. It has also allowed us to look outwardly at the oppressive and inequitable schooling conditions created by those who ultimately shape American education. As educational leaders, we are also unbecoming perpetuators of racist school policies and practices that create an inequality of education. In our unbecoming, we are beginning to understand why multicultural education is a reform movement based on equality of education.

In trying to understand how educational leaders would receive the critical chapters we have compiled, a group of educational leaders used the manuscript as a primary text for a doctoral course. During one of the sessions, a student pointed out that the readings were a bit offensive to her as a Black woman and wondered how White school leaders dealt with the powerful language that she described as *inflammatory*. Several students countered that a kinder, gentler language would skirt around the real magnitude of the crisis facing non-White students. What was needed, according to one student, was the straight talk embodied in this book.

The dynamic discourse that took place in this class session forced us to think more deeply about how educational leaders would receive the book. After an additional review, a decision was made to keep the language in a form that would capture the magnitude of the educational crisis impacting non-White students. However, we did not take lightly the comments of the offended student, who also noted that she did not find anything untrue in the book. We realized that we were indeed at a crossroads, and while perhaps the book could not satisfy varying perspectives about its language, for educational leaders who are aware that something is wrong with the schooling and education of non-White students the book will probably draw *amen* from the chorus of leaders who are in a precarious position of trying to do good but find their efforts being curtailed by policies that are making schools dead zones, meaning that the spontaneity and joy of learning is sidelined for *technocratic rigor, stiffness* and *death*. So in a way the book champions the frustrations of conscientious educational leaders.

In summary, the multicultural education that we present in this book is not a feel-good approach that deals with sharing cultural dishes, artifacts, or other symbols that do not address the systemic issues of inequality in education. We address systemic issues using a critical educational theory approach to multicultural education. The candid conversations are indeed *straight talk*. Our hope is to *trouble the waters* that have allowed some educational leaders to turn a blind eye to the racist and oppressive schooling conditions that too many students encounter. If you can bear this reading, you may very well be on your way to becoming an educational leader that will change the course of history.

REFERENCES

Freire, P. (2000). *Pedagogy of the oppressed*. New York: Continuum.

Paige, R., & E. Witty. (2010). *The Black-White achievement gap: Why closing it is the greatest civil rights issue of our time*. AMACOM.

Shields, C. (Ed.). (2011). Transformative leadership: An introduction. In C. Shields (Ed.), *Transformative leadership in education* (pp. 1–17). New York: Peter Lang.

Introduction

Critical Race Theory for Educational Leaders

Abul Pitre

A few years ago during a summer semester, a group of educational leaders took a course titled Cultural Diversity in American Education, and as part of the culminating class project, students were required to write a publishable paper that could later be turned into a book. However, because the course lasted only four weeks, the students were unable to complete their final papers. Despite its short length, the course covered several major topics, including race, racism, social class, special needs, religion, and gender issues.

Several class sessions seemed to alarm some students, creating what might be termed a *crisis*, and it was exacerbated when the topic of racism and critical pedagogy were the center of discussion. Students were troubled by the ways racism and social class inequities were perpetuated in schools, and through deeper reading and reflecting on their work as school leaders, they began to see the depth of the systemic inequities permeating educational institutions.

The following semester, the same educational leaders were engaged in a course titled Legal and Ethical Issues. During the course of the class, an epiphany occurred through the text, *Foundations of Critical Race Theory in Education*, which seemed to summarize the conversations from the previous semester's diversity course. Amazingly, the students had come to realize that *race does matter in schools*.

As a follow-through on the agreement to write a book on educational leaders and multicultural education, they soon completed preliminary drafts. Initially the book was titled *Multicultural Education for Educational Leaders*; however, as the articles were edited, it became apparent that the students

1

had produced something extraordinary during their research on multicultural education, adding a rare but much-needed perspective for school leaders. The book's title became *Multicultural Education for Educational Leaders: Critical Race Theory and Antiracist Perspectives.*

In his book *Race Matters*, Cornel West highlights the significance of race in American society. He argues, "To engage in a serious discussion of race in America, we must begin not with the problems of [B]lack people but with the flaws of American society—flaws rooted in historic inequalities and long-standing cultural stereotypes" (p. 53). A major flaw in American society can be traced back to its educational process, which has had a "double consciousness." In his book, *Mis-education of the Negro*, Carter G. Woodson (1933/ 2008) wrote on *double consciousness*: "The same educational process which inspires and stimulates the oppressor with the thought that he is everything and has accomplished everything worthwhile, depresses and crushes at the same time the spark of genius in the Negro making him feel that his race does not amount to much and never will measure up to the standards of other people" (xiii).

With all of the current educational debate focusing on the inequitable schooling experience of non-White students and the existence of the so-called achievement gap, there remains a great deal of misunderstanding, and perhaps even denial. History has shown that "the conditions of today have been determined by what has happened in the past" (Woodson, 1933/2008, p. 9). Thus, if we are to move forward in the creation of a balanced education system, we must accept that at the center of American life are the issues of race and racism; racism is as American as apple pie.

It could be argued that one of the primary reasons race has continued to play a major part in the American landscape is because the overarching educational system reinforces White supremacy. This ideology has shaped curricula, student-teacher interaction, school policies, and community relations, to mention a few. To effectively dismantle racism in the American educational system, a complete overhaul of the current system is a must.

Colleges of education would have to be at the forefront of this paradigm shift because the death of racism would require teacher educators and educational leaders to be prepared to undertake a critical study of the social order and the schools' role in shaping that order. Educational leaders should serve as visionaries, but what happens when those would-be leaders enter graduate programs that are primarily focused on teaching skill sets?

In describing the educational leadership dilemma, Lopez (2003) writes, "The important stuff in educational leadership is not about creating schools that work for all children but rest in the more technical matters of school finance, organizational theory, leadership theory, and other staple topics" (p. 70). This type of vocational training produces commissar administrators who seek to maintain the existing order as opposed to producing school leaders who transform schools into just, equitable, and powerful catalysts for social change.

While most colleges of education are accustomed to facing accreditation issues related to diversity, educational leadership programs have been able to skirt specific diversity issues regarding race and racism. Though progress in addressing diversity remains stagnant at an additive approach, some colleges of education have been compelled to offer courses that address multicultural education. Moreover, some teacher education programs offer courses solely focused on the topic of racism; for example, a major Midwestern university offers a course titled Race and Inequality in American Education, and another major West Coast university at one time offered a course titled Pedagogy of Malcolm X. Additionally, some urban education programs also address issues related to race and racism. However, for the vast majority of students in educational leadership programs, there seems to be minimal discussion about racism.

If in a room of educators and a discussion about eliminating racism ensued, most educational leaders would be disturbed by the discourse, as evidenced by a recent meeting of educational administrators where a participant suggested changing the admission requirements for an educational leadership program. The proposed change would eliminate the program's process of self-nomination and require an administrator to nominate potential candidates into the Master of School Administration program.

When questioned about available mechanisms to ensure diversity in the applicant pool, one Black superintendent responded, "I don't look for diversity; I look for people who can do the job." This comment and others made it apparent that administrators across the country may share this Eurocentric thinking, which contributes to the structure of White supremacist schools.

The few non-Whites who do enter into administrative positions may have fulfilled Woodson's (1933/2008) prophetic utterance regarding the education of African Americans.

> With mis-educated Negroes in control themselves, however, it is doubtful that the system would be very much different from what it is or that it would rapidly undergo change. The Negroes thus placed in charge would be the products of the same system and would show no more conception of the task at hand than do the Whites who have educated them and shaped their minds as they would have them function. (p. 23)

Educational leaders and the programs that have shaped their thinking do not allow for critical dialogue that could be transformative. In this book, you will find compelling reasons for why educational leaders need to engage in critical race theory and antiracist conversations in their graduate programs. If the vast majority of educational leaders are trained in postsecondary programs that do not address racism, it is highly likely that racism will continue to be perpetuated in America's schools.

UNDERSTANDING CRITICAL RACE THEORY

In 1995, Ladson-Billings and Tate wrote one of the first major papers on the idea of critical race theory in education. In a subsequent book titled *Critical Race Theory Perspectives on Social Studies* (2003), Ladson-Billings, along with other teacher educators, specifically discuss the pervasiveness of race in the teaching of social studies. The author writes, "And for the purpose of this discussion I want to suggest that race is an ever-present concept in the social studies—in the curriculum, the profession, and its policies and practices" (p. 2). Similarly, the issue of race and racism should be an important topic of study in the area of educational leadership.

Educational leaders and leadership programs should form the bedrock for issues related to race and racism in schools. Historically, educational leaders are shaped or birthed into a profession that is dominated by Whiteness. The vast majority of school leaders in this country are White. In addition, an examination of the racial dynamics of school boards might result in the surprising find that in some cases the school board is majority White even though the student population is majority non-White, leaving the educational decisions of Black and minority students in the hands of people outside their race.

Another factor worth exploring is the race of leaders in state departments of education. The selection of these leaders reveals that beyond the local school and school board is the state legislature, which is a major player in determining how schools will operate in a particular state. Examining state legislatures will result in the finding that the majority of state legislatures are again White. The problem is not skin color as such but the ideology that has historically embodied these lawmaking sanctuaries and the people who work in them.

All of these factors play a significant role in revealing the need for critical race theory in educational leadership. Lopez (2003) argues, "Quite simply, preparation programs across the nation do very little to equip students with a cogent understanding of racism and race relations. Moreover, when these topics are introduced, they are often relegated to special topics courses or seminars that are not a part of the core curriculum of leadership preparation" (p. 70).

HISTORY OF CRITICAL RACE THEORY IN EDUCATION

Understanding the origin of critical race theory is significant, so let us briefly consider it and its application for educational leaders. Critical race theory (CRT) has emerged to inform our understanding of race and education. CRT is primarily concerned with race and its impact on American life. Ladson-Billings (2003) notes the origin of CRT: "Critical race theory sprang up in the mid-1970s with the early work of legal scholar Derrick Bell and Alan Freeman, both of whom were distressed over the slow pace of racial reform in the United States" (p. 8).

CRT considers racism to be a normal part of American life. More importantly, critical race theorists seek to expose racism and its impact on American life. Gollnick and Chinn (2012) point out that CRT "focuses on racism in challenging racial oppression, racial inequities, and White privilege" (p. 28).

Stovall (2005) identifies two major aspects of CRT as educational protest and scholarship. More importantly, Stovall links CRT to identification of White supremacy in education and methods used to eradicate its dominance in education. For the most part, racism is everywhere in the education world, and educational leaders, the people who could play a major role in dismantling it, are not cognizant of its existence.

In the courses that became the basis for this book, the initial class sessions were designed to test these educational leaders' knowledge of racism in educational settings. The conversation began in an organizational theory and cultural diversity course that lent itself to the discussion of racism. Using Nieto and Bode's (2012) framework in *Affirming Diversity*, it was amazing that these educational leaders had never thought about racism to this degree.

Nieto and Bode (2012) define racism as prejudice plus power, and they point out two forms of racism: individual racism and institutional racism. They contend, "Although the beliefs and behaviors of individuals may be very hurtful and psychologically damaging, institutional discrimination— that is, the systematic use of economic and political power in institutions (such as schools) that leads to detrimental policies and practices—does far greater damage" (p. 64). This argument suggests that it is necessary for educational leaders to understand racial inequality and its systematic inherency in school policy and practice.

While having these conversations about race and racism, some of the educational leaders had difficulty comprehending how schools produce race and social class inequalities. One leader, a White female who wrote chapter 3, had grown up in the Midwest region of the United States and could not understand Nieto and Bode's argument to dismantle tracking. She argued that tracking was necessary, but as she begin to speak more about her experiences it became clear that she could not grasp the concept of tracking and racism because she had never been around people outside of her race in a meaningful way. Her first real encounter with Black people came as result of being placed in a majority Black school as a teacher, an experience of which she expressed, "I was terrified."

In addition to using Nieto and Bode's framework of the sociopolitical nature of multicultural education, the course embedded elements of Asante's "Afrocentric Idea." Prior to assigning Asante's reading, students were required to develop some understanding of the historical issues that gave birth to multicultural education. Even more importantly, the course was designed to take the students on a historical journey to the period when the first Blacks arrived in America to be made slaves. They were required to read *The Willie Lynch Letter and the Making of Slaves* (Hassan-EL, 2007), a work that has been argued is a fabrication but nonetheless created shock for the educational leaders. They began to see elements of Lynch's ideas being played out in the educational arena. At this point they began to ask questions and make comments, like,

> If Lynch was right about the sustainability of his conditioning process, then educators of today must realize their responsibility to make changes and end the process. Lynch makes it clear that "values are created and transported by communication through the body of the language. A total society has many interconnected value systems." Educational leaders should heed his message, and begin to use his method for positive efforts towards racial unity and acceptance. This concept validates the importance of spreading multicultural education across the curriculum so that the underlying values can be instilled in more deep and meaningful ways.

Regarding its application for educational leaders, one student wrote:

> It is important for this letter to be read and taught to school-aged children so they can begin to understand the construct of the Black individual, family, and community. I believe it is particularly important for Black children to understand this letter. Educational leaders are in some ways being controlled by not having the flexibility to teach certain material and content. It is highly unlikely that this material will be taught in detail to K–12 or even to college-level students, but it should be taught in the home and in the community. As an educational leader, this letter has allowed me to look through a different lens within my own educational system. I began to count the number of Black upper-level managers within my Institution. There are three Black directors (to include myself), one assistant VP, and one VP in a total of 200 full-time employees. How does this happen? I have noticed this issue in the past, but this letter has made me more aware of the fact. It's quite unsettling yet motivating at the same time. This is a paradox that will force me to continue moving in a direction of empowerment by educating myself to help others.

It could be argued that what is needed in conjunction with CRT is a component that could be called Black Studies for Educational Leaders. Asante (1991) argues, "Multicultural education is thus a fundamental necessity for anyone who wishes to achieve competency in almost any subject. . . . The Afrocentric idea must be the stepping stone from which the multicultural idea is launched" (p. 172).

Asante's ideas for Afrocentricity as the launching for multicultural education would be especially important for educational leaders who may have historical amnesia. Because the overwhelming number of schools that are considered failing are predominately Black and Hispanic, this requires educational leaders to have some understanding of the historical plight of these groups. Black studies could provide a stimulus for ameliorating the problem addressed by Butterfield: "Knowledge of the sins of the fathers is a terrible burden for the children of pirates, murderers, kidnappers, rapists, for the children of those who received the benefits of stolen labor and genocide and closed their eyes, perhaps with humanitarian shudder, to its effects" (cited in Pinar, 2004, p. 41).

This is a point where educational leaders would have to face the demons that have haunted the sociopolitical nature of education. Historically, confronting this truth has been very difficult for educators, and I suppose it is even more daunting for those leaders who have played a role in the deep forgetting described by Pinar (2004), in what he calls an *official story*:

> The official story a nation or culture tells itself—often evident in school curriculum—hides other truths. The national story also creates the illusion of truth being on the social surface, when it is nearly axiomatic that the stories we tell ourselves mask the unacceptable truths. What we as a nation try not to remember—genocide, slavery, lynching, prison rape—structures the politics of our collective identification and imagined affiliation. (p. 38)

Pinar's disclosure of the official story was evidenced in events described in *Freedom Fighters: Struggles Instituting the Study of Black History in K–12 Education* (Pitre, 2011). The book details how CRT played out in the context of a school's Black history program that became controversial when a few White teachers walked out. One of the White teachers who disagreed with the contents of the guest speaker's address is believed to have phoned the school board to intercede on behalf of the student unrest that he perceived would take place as a result of the Black history program.

The next day, the majority White school leadership of the central office, along with sheriff's deputies, descended on the majority Black school. One of the major underpinnings in the book was that it used a case study and student interviews illuminating the role of racism, privilege, and White supremacy in school. In the case study, concerned parents pointed out that "racism was and is the basis used in past historical events that caused races to be intimidated and deprived of human dignity" (Pitre, 2011). The head of the NAACP also discussed the institutional role of racism in this particular school district, noting the role of the educational leaders: "The system is racist for allowing those types of things to happen. . . . We met with the superintendent last year about White teachers leading White students out of those programs. We approached the superintendent a week prior to the assembly and asked that a policy be established" (p. 2).

The study also made the connection between CRT and White privilege, which was clearly observed in the case study and student narratives. This privilege was manifested as some teachers who walked out of the program did so knowing they would not be reprimanded; indeed, walking out of Black history programs had been an ongoing phenomenon prior to this particular incident. White privilege was illuminated when White school administrators showed up the day after the program with sheriff's deputies—a show of force that has been attributed to one teacher who phoned the school board indicating there would be violence at the school.

The privilege of being White afforded these teachers with a level of comfort that paved the way for them to openly display racist attitudes. In fact, one teacher had the audacity to tell the Black students he felt bad for them because they had to hear another Black person talk like that. Perhaps more insulting and illuminating was the ensuing apology by the school principal, who was forced by the Whites in power to hold an assembly apologizing for the Black history program. This apology crystallized the racism, power, and privilege afforded to those in the dominant group.

The Black history program, despite being a powerful tool for constructive change among the students, was seen as threatening to the majority White school leaders and prompted parents to form a group called the Concerned Parents Organization that challenged the practice of racism at the school. In a letter to the local newspaper, the parents pointed out, "We have some racist teachers in our public schools, those who send their children to private schools because a Black teacher isn't good enough to teach their children but they teach ours" (Pitre, 2011, p. 39). The parents in this study were in the forefront of identifying and challenging the unjust and inequitable school policies in this school district.

The students were also very active in this challenge, displaying their anger by walking out of school for several days and attending school board meetings to protest the board's decisions. The students' protest demonstrated a newfound consciousness of the individual and institutional racism. What seemed to emerge was that the students were protesting against a system that had sought to reduce them to beings for others. They realized that they had been made victims of what Freire (2000) called "domestication" and Woodson (2008) called "mis-education."

Educational leaders who are exposed to CRT as a component of Black studies could have a powerful impact on transforming schools. In the aforementioned study, leaders could have used the situation at this particular school to create a very powerful opportunity to eradicate racism and inequality in schools. However, blinded by what Howard (2006) describes as the *luxury of ignorance* and the *White is right assumption*, these school leaders instead revealed the racist ideologies that have historically impeded non-White students' quests for equality of education.

Howard (2006) writes, "This was real colorblindness: Whites seeing only in White . . . The luxury of selective forgetting is not afforded to those who have suffered the consequences of White dominance. For them, the American Dream has often become an unbearable nightmare. . . . Through the luxury of ignorance, Whites for centuries maintained a view of reality that 'makes sense' to us [Whites]" (p. 63).

Peter McLaren (2015) cogently asserts, "The specific struggle that I wish to address is that of choosing against Whiteness . . . My message is that we must create a new public sphere where the practice of Whiteness is not only identified but also contested and destroyed" (p. 261). What better place to start contesting racism than with the educational leaders who have the power to steer us onto new roads that bring us beyond the rhetoric of equality into the confines of the school where justice and equality could reign supreme?

OVERVIEW OF THE BOOK

In this book are eight chapters by educators who reflect on issues pertinent to multicultural education and racism. Chapter 1 discusses the changing demographics of public schools, the definition of multicultural education, and the need for school leaders to embrace concepts found in multicultural education.

Chapter 2 tackles the role of multicultural education in predominantly Black schools. Contrasting ideas about multicultural education as the sharing of artifacts, or what Banks (2014) calls the *additive approach*, the authors contend that the sociopolitical aspects of multicultural education should be applied to majority Black schools. The chapter highlights the oppressive and punitive policies that negatively impact Black students and proposes multicultural education as a way for school leaders to transform schools for Black students.

The author of chapter 3 uses a critical White studies framework to reflect on the experiences of a White educational leader who had limited interactions with people of color, particularly Blacks. The author describes this White educator's experiences in a doctoral program that awakened her to the systemic racism that pervades public schools and concludes that educational leaders *can't lead students they don't know*.

In chapter 4, multicultural education, the curriculum, and the impact of White teachers are reviewed from a theoretical framework grounded in White studies. The chapter illuminates the role that teachers play in determining how the curriculum is experienced, calling into question the cultural incongruence that may exist between White teachers and students of color. Educational leaders are provided with critical insights about possible reasons that non-White students may not do as well on high-stakes end-of-grade exams.

Chapter 5 introduces a new theoretical framework coined *critical Black pedagogy in education*, an approach that suggests there is a need to revisit the educational ideas of Black leaders. Chapter 6 draws on the impact of unequal funding and how it impacts student achievement. The author compares and contrasts two different schools in the same district, one in an affluent area and the other in a poor area. What he discloses are the *savage inequalities* described in Jonathan Kozol's ethnographic research.

Chapter 7 examines institutional racism in higher education. The author highlights the necessity of critical pedagogy for leaders in K–12 and higher-education settings and examines the work of Elijah Muhammad as part of the overall deconstruction of Whiteness through the use of critical pedagogy and multicultural education. The chapter concludes with a summary about how to best eradicate racism in educational institutions.

Chapter 8 addresses multicultural education as an ethical, moral, and social justice imperative for school leaders, challenging leaders to dismantle the inequities that exist in schools and critiquing current school leadership practices.

REFERENCES

Asante, M. (1991). The Afrocentric idea in education. *Journal of Negro Education* 60, no. 2: 170–80.

Banks, J. A. (2014). *An introduction to multicultural education* (5th ed.). Boston: Pearson.

Freire, P. (2000). *Pedagogy of the oppressed*. New York: Continuum.

Gollnick, D., & P. Chinn. (2012). *Multicultural education in a pluralistic society* (9th ed.). Upper Saddle River, NJ: Pearson Education, Inc.

Hassan-EL, K. (2007). *The Willie Lynch letter and the making of slaves*. Besenville, IL: Lushena Books.

Howard, G. (2006). *We can't teach what we don't know: White teachers in multiracial schools* (2nd ed.). New York: Teachers College Press.

Ladson-Billings, G. (2003). Lies my teacher still tells: Developing a critical race theory perspective toward the social studies. In G. Ladson-Billings (Ed.), *Critical race theory perspectives on social studies: The profession, policies, and curriculum* (pp. 1–14). Greenwich, CT: Information Age Publishers.

Ladson-Billings, G., & W. Tate. (1995). Toward a critical race theory of education. *Teachers College Record* 97, no. 1: 47–68.

Lopez, G. (2003). The (racially neutral) politics of education: A critical race theory perspective. *Educational Administration Quarterly* 39: 68–94.

McLaren, P. (2015). *Life in schools: An introduction to critical pedagogy in the foundations of education* (6th ed.). Boulder: Paradigm.

Nieto, S., & P. Bode. (2012). *Affirming diversity: The sociopolitical context of multicultural education* (6th ed.). Boston: Allyn and Bacon.

Pinar, W. (2004). *What is curriculum theory?* (2nd ed.). Mahwah, NJ: Lawrence Erlbaum Associates.

Pitre, A. (2011). *Freedom fighters: Struggles instituting the study of Black history in K–12 education.* San Francisco, CA: Cognella.

Stovall, D. (2005). Critical race theory as educational protest: Power and praxis. In W. Watkins (Ed.), *Black protest thought and education* (pp. 197–211). Oxford: Peter Lang Publishers.

West, C. (1993). *Race matters*. New York: Beacon Press.

Woodson, C. G. (1933/2008). *The mis-education of the Negro*. Drewryville, VA: Kha Books.

Chapter One

Preparing School Leaders to Understand Multicultural Education

Judith Douglas

INTRODUCTION

It is of great necessity that school leaders align public institutions to meet the needs of diverse student populations, creating a new paradigm for the twenty-first-century learner. Schools must address the rapidly changing world, which is racially, ethnically, religiously, and linguistically diverse. Although schools are working to meet the demands of technology advances, teacher retention, and other issues related to student achievement, they have remained insufficient when it comes to serving historically marginalized students.

One of the major goals of multicultural education is to ensure that "all students regardless of their gender, sexual orientation, social class, and ethnic, racial or cultural characteristics should have an equal opportunity to learn" (Banks, 2014, p. 1). Thus, school leaders play a pivotal role in ensuring that schools afford all children opportunities to be successful. As the United States continues to experience a population shift, it becomes increasingly important for school leaders to understand the need for multicultural education. In the South where 38 percent of the U.S. population is educated, students of color make up the majority of those attending public schools (Oakes & Lipton, 2007; Suitts, 2010).

Banks (2014) highlights this phenomenon when he says, "The percentage of students of color in U.S. public schools has doubled in the 30 years between 1973 and 2004, growing from 22 to 43 percent of the school population" (p. ix). Even more significant is the prediction that by the year 2050 Whites will no longer be the majority population in America (Yen, 2009).

What does this mean for school leaders? Ultimately, it means that school leaders will need to be immersed in multicultural education concepts prior to assuming leadership roles in schools.

Unfortunately, the sad reality is that school leaders are more than likely unprepared to address multicultural education in public schools. Trained in administrator programs that scantly offer courses in multicultural education, school leaders may unknowingly be perpetuating the unjust, cyclical nature of public schooling. For a vast number of public schools, education has thus far not reflected the needs of the new, diverse majority in public schools; instead, the Anglocentric curriculum still exists in "varying degrees in the nation's schools" (Banks, 2014, p. 3).

Even more daunting is that school leaders are inadequately prepared to address multicultural education from a sociopolitical perspective that uses critical theories to dissect leadership, teaching, and learning. Nieto and Bode (2012), highlighting the sociopolitical construct of multicultural education, point out that it is antiracist, basic education, and is a pervasive process important for social justice, critical pedagogy, and for all students.

These critical areas of multicultural education present twenty-first-century school leaders with the daunting responsibility of deconstructing the traditional approaches to education that have ill served students of various races, religions, social classes, and ethnic groups. A major hurdle for these leaders will be how well they can construct a new educational system that truly empowers all students. This will require them to work with parents and local communities in dismantling the traditional Eurocentered school system, and one of the first steps in the process is advocating for multicultural education.

School leaders are the key to ensuring the implementation of multicultural education in schools, but they must first understand it and know why it is needed. This chapter contends that there are several reasons for school leaders to address multicultural education. Among the concerns this chapter will address are the changing demographics of the U.S. population, the history of multicultural education, and the legacy of White dominance. The chapter concludes by offering ways leaders can be prepared to implement multicultural education in their schools.

CHANGING DEMOGRAPHICS OF THE UNITED STATES

America's public schools have become increasingly diverse in terms of linguistic, religious, racial, and ethnic groups. A historical precursor provides a good example of the emerging diversity that compares the 1970s to the era in which we now live. In 1970, when the baby boomers were enrolled in elementary and high school, the student population was 79 percent White, 14 percent Black, 6 percent Hispanic, and 1 percent Asian/Pacific Islander and other races. In 2003, however, 60 percent were White, 18 percent Hispanic, 16 percent Black, and 4 percent Asian/Pacific Islander.

The U.S. Census Bureau's projections through 2050 indicate significant growth among all non-White populations in the United States and predict that by 2050, Whites will no longer be the majority (Yen, 2009). The Hispanic population will grow from 35.6 to 102.6 million, or 188 percent, nearly doubling its share of the nation's population from 12.6 percent in 2000 to 24.4 percent. The Asian population will grow 213 percent, or from 10.7 to 33.4 million, more than doubling its share of the population from 3.8 percent to 8 percent. The Black population is expected to increase from 35.8 to 61.4 million, or 71 percent—an overall U.S. population increase to 14.6 percent from 12.7 percent.

Meanwhile, the non-Hispanic White population will increase by only 7 percent, from 195.7 to 210.3 million, or an overall U.S. population decline from 69.4 percent in 2000 to 50.1 percent in 2050.

America's racial and ethnic diversity is not the only demographic change; religious diversity is also growing. Islam is among the fastest-growing religions in the United States, and the majority of its converts, particularly in the urban centers of the country, are Black (Banks, 2014).

These changing demographics are of great significance considering the fact that American educators are predominantly White Christians. Politically speaking, the control over school operations primarily belongs to Whites in positions of power. School leaders will be challenged to make a paradigm shift in operations and develop new competencies, pedagogies, philosophies, and leadership styles to successfully meet the needs of the diverse population. Banks (2014) writes, "The extent to which these challenges will be transformed into opportunities will depend largely on the vision, knowledge, and commitment of each nation's educators. You will have to take a stand on multicultural education and determine what actions related to it you will take in your classroom and school" (p. 16).

Unfortunately, most school leaders are being prepared to work from a scientific management model that does not include multicultural education. This, along with the plethora of White males occupying a majority of the school administrative positions, suggests a compelling need for colleges of education to reorganize their administration programs to address multicultural education from a sociopolitical perspective.

HISTORICAL DEVELOPMENT

Multicultural education grew out of the civil rights movement of the 1950s and 1960s, the latter of which witnessed student protest in public schools and college campuses across the United States. Students in both institutions protested what they saw as racist structures that denied students of color equal opportunities for success. One of the major changes in American education came about as a result of the *Brown v. Board of Education* ruling that required schools to desegregate with all deliberate speed and consequently brought about the closing of several Black schools.

Black educators were fired, displaced, and eventually run out of the profession. Many were no longer able to circumvent or deflect the racist curricula (Jenkins, 2009). Black students were suddenly at the mercy of White educators. Decades earlier, Woodson eloquently described the dilemma inherent in Black education when he argued that "the education of the Negroes, then, the most important thing in the uplift of the Negroes, is almost entirely in the hands of those who have enslaved them and now segregate them" (2008, p. 22). Woodson's articulation of Black education in the 1930s was a forerunner to both the Black educational landscape of the 1960s and the current multicultural education movement.

In tracing the origin of multicultural education, Banks writes, "Woodson probably did more than any other individual to promote the study and teaching of African American history in the nation's schools and colleges" (2001, p. 7). Further, he averred that "the current multicultural education movement is directly linked to the early ethnic studies movement initiated by individuals such as Du Bois (1935), Woodson (1919/1968), Bond (1939), and Wesley (1935)" (p. 10). The monumental work of these educators in advancing multicultural education is virtually unknown among school leaders, however, as they have not been exposed to these scholars.

Multicultural education also grew out of the demands of ethnic groups for inclusion in the curricula of schools, colleges, and universities; it is an outgrowth of ethnic education prior to the 1960s. Banks (2005) writes, "Policies and programs in ethnic education did not suddenly arise during the ethnic revitalization movements of the 1960s and 1970s. These developments evolved gradually over a long period" (p. 42).

When ethnic studies education was revived in the 1960s, African Americans and other ethnic groups refused to acquiesce to demands to renounce their cultural identity and heritage. They insisted that their lives and histories be included in the educational curricula. In challenging the dominant paradigms and concepts taught in schools and colleges, multicultural educators sought to transform the Eurocentric perspective and incorporate multiple perspectives into the curricula.

Educational institutions and organizations were pushed to address the concerns of marginalized groups, and those concerns were primarily focused on making additions to the traditional school curriculum. The 1980s saw the emergence of a body of scholarship on multicultural education by progressive educational activists and researchers who refused to allow schools to simply add token programs and special units on famous people of color.

By the mid to late 1980s, scholars such as James Banks, Carl Grant, Christine Sleeter, Geneva Gay, Gary Howard, and Sonia Nieto had provided significant scholarship in multicultural education that served to develop new and deeper frameworks grounded in the ideal of equal opportunity and a connection between school transformation and social change. They shifted the multicultural education focus from the mere inclusion of ethnic content to deep structural school changes. During these years, multicultural educators also expanded the focus on ethnic groups of color to other group categories such as social class, language, and gender.

Although conceptually distinct, the key social categories of multicultural education—race, class, gender, and culture—are interrelated. Multicultural theorists are concerned with how these social variables interact in identity formation and the consequences of multiple and contextual identities for teaching and learning.

More importantly, they are concerned with how these variables may operate in perpetuating unequal schooling opportunities for students of color. As a result, multicultural scholars address racism, social class, religion, special education, language, and gender issues in education. In many regards they can be seen as social activists advocating for equal educational opportunities for students who are marginalized and oppressed in schools.

Their work challenges school leaders to examine power relations in schools and work to truly become leaders by providing students with an education that empowers them to make changes in the larger society. Multicultural concepts espouse tenets that can be challenging to the scientific management approach to education that is built on White supremacy.

Contrary to school leaders, who are trained in programs that depict leadership as being detached from human experience, multicultural scholars argue for a human relations approach to understanding leadership. They contend that school leaders should work to dismantle the oppressive and inequitable systemic structures that leave some children behind. The sociopolitical context of multicultural education is ideologically opposite from the preparation of school leaders who are in too many cases commissars for the real owners of the schools.

Too often the term *leader* as it relates to public schools does not really depict leadership in the sense that school leaders are coerced to maintain oppressive school structures. Freire (2000) argues insightfully in *Pedagogy of the Oppressed* that educators must be comrades in the students' struggle to create a society free from oppressive conditions that too many live under. The tenets espoused by Freire form a foundation for what is called critical pedagogy.

Critical pedagogy is an examination of the relationship between power and knowledge. School leaders are in dire need of courses that allow them to study critical pedagogy in order to gain access to knowledge that will allow them to really be leaders. Some historical Black school leaders exemplified the tenets of critical pedagogy as witnessed by their ability to engage students, parents, and communities in ways that empowered these groups. To follow their example, critical pedagogue school leaders must ask this question: With the new majority in public schools, how will those in power see the education of students of color?

In the past, those in power constructed schools that fit the needs of their interest. In *The White Architects of Black Education*, Watkins (2001) surmises how these powerful philanthropists developed an educational system that would make Blacks subservient, docile, and mis-educated. Will the architects of twenty-first-century education espouse a similar agenda? Cloaked under the premise of equality, the No Child Left Behind Act of 2001 and Race to the Top have actually resulted in more students being left behind.

Pitre (2009) contends that new legislation using high-stakes testing is the right arm of White supremacist thinking, while Gabbard and Ross (2004) argue that the new legislation has resulted in the privatization of schools, which is in the interest of large corporations. McLaren (2015) highlights the former Bush administration's connection with textbook publishers and the huge sums of money generated through that relationship under the disguise of leaving no child left behind. School leaders studying critical pedagogy, a tenet of multicultural education, offer a great possibility for creating schools that will truly educate all students. In the next section, the definition of multicultural education is discussed in the hope that it will provide school leaders with a framework to develop educational practices that empower students, teachers, parents, and communities.

DEFINING MULTICULTURAL EDUCATION

James A. Banks (2014), who has been called the "father of multicultural education," defines *multicultural education* as "an idea or concept, an educational reform movement and a process" (p. 1).

A prerequisite for multicultural education is a need for diverse perspectives to be included in the curriculum. This means school leaders should address several major areas such as policy statements, staff attitudes, the curriculum, teaching materials and strategies, parent participation, and the racial makeup of the school faculty and staff (Banks, 2014). In the aforementioned strands, school leaders need to ensure that multicultural education is a persistent thread. Its inclusion in the overall school program is needed to eradicate racism from the institutional structures in schools (Nieto & Bode, 2012).

Racism in the United States has created an educational system that continues to ignore the culture of students of color. One of the ways racism has persisted is through tracking; students of color are relegated to the lower tracks where teaching and pedagogy are based on rote memorization (Nieto & Bode, 2012). Pitre (2009) argued that racism still exists in schools as a result of tracking: "In this type of setting, White supremacy may become rooted in the subconscious minds of both Black and White students" (p. vii).

An aim of multicultural education is to help educators see the necessity of working to dismantle racism in both the school and the larger society (Nieto & Bode, 2012). Multicultural education is not an occasional study of a famous personality or holiday that leaves out untold stories while keeping the Anglo-Saxon perspective and unjust school policies intact.

The "tokenism" concept, a practice of making a token effort to minorities, can be found in school policies, practices, and the curriculum. Many of the schools' efforts toward multicultural education are what Banks calls additive approaches that do not address the systemic issues that have made schools and society unequal. Cultural diversity seems to be nothing more than a token effort: a bulletin board display of famous Black Americans during Black History Month, a morning message about Hispanic Heritage Month or Native American History Month, or the reading of a Hanukkah or a Kwanzaa book during religious holidays.

While multicultural scholars would welcome these efforts, they would ask deeper questions about the racist school curricula, the overrepresentation of Black males in special education, zero-tolerance policies, teacher expectations for students of color, diversity of the faculty and staff, and high-stakes testing, to name a few.

Banks (2014) explains that there are four orientations to transforming curriculum to multicultural education: the contributions, additive, transformative, and the social action approach. Celebrating Martin Luther King Day would be an example of the contributions approach, while an additive approach would be to add good books, such as *The Watsons Go to Birmingham* (Christopher Paul Curtis, 1963; appropriate for sixth-grade students), to the existing curriculum. According to Banks, the transformative approach is better because it helps children look at reality differently, but the best option is the social action approach, where students are engaged in making decisions on important social issues and taking action to help solve those issues.

Transforming curriculum goes beyond additive and contributive approaches to diversity because these only add to what is already there but do not change the perspective. Multicultural education challenges, disrupts, and reinterprets content, concepts, and paradigms from the established curriculum. Multicultural education is about cultural pluralism—truth telling that paints an accurate picture of the total human experience no matter what events we choose to examine. Banks (2014) cogently explains,

> Although multicultural education is not against the West, its theorists believe
> that the truth about the West should be told, that its debt to people of color and
> women be recognized and included in the curriculum, and that the discrepan-
> cies between the ideals of freedom and equality and the realities of racism and
> sexism be taught to students. (p. 11)

American culture has been persistently referred to as a mythological "melting pot," a concept dating back to the early twentieth century. One would think the concept was formulated on the premise that immigrant cultures, religions, and ethnic groups would "mix" into a new culture; however, the mixing was jaded and its evolution involved various groups having to assimilate to the dominant culture and in the process abandoning many of their traditions and characteristics. This is contrary to multicultural education, where one acknowledges differences and does not attempt to make "one size fit all."

To effectively implement multicultural education, school leaders need to see it as a reform movement that permeates every aspect of the educational community. As schools become more diverse, it is the responsibility of leaders to find the most effective ways to help all students succeed academically and to provide students with knowledge of self and others while maintaining respect for all people.

School leaders must also make sure they are well prepared to lead in a multicultural society. Awareness of multicultural education concepts is wasted energy if it does not provoke praxis, or reflection on the problems in school and consequent development of an action plan to solve those problems. Education is about growing; growth occurs through changed thinking and seeking different "lenses" to see problems through a new perspective.

WHITE DOMINANCE AND WHITE PRIVILEGE

If schools are to be examined as social systems and multicultural education is to be understood as an effort toward educational equality and social justice, it is necessary to understand the social structures that have existed and perpetuated injustices. One of the ways that inequalities have been able to exist is through the legacy of dominance and White privilege. Historically, America's framers viewed the world from a monocultural perspective that allowed them to dominate non-White groups. What emerged from that dominance was a culture of White supremacy that was embedded into every U.S. institution. Even lower-class Whites, despite being used by the ruling elite, were given special privileges based on their race—White privilege.

Education was the social vehicle that embodied the ideas of White supremacist logic. Scholars such as John Dewey acknowledged the power of education and how the school could be used as a vehicle for social reform. As one of the leading and most influential educational theorists, Dewey believed in a progressive approach to education. He believed there is an intimate connection between education and social action in a democracy, writing that democracy has to be born in each generation (Dewey, 1889).

Similarly, in his *Mis-Education of the Negro*, Woodson saw education as a vehicle for social reform and challenged the White supremacist education that Blacks received in a way similar to critical pedagogues. W. E. B. Du Bois also envisioned an education for Blacks that would create a different society—one in which Blacks would be empowered to control their own destiny. These scholars espoused several of the ideas of multicultural education as a reform movement that would dislodge the inequalities that exist in schools. To effectively address these inequalities, White dominance should be viewed in light of the term *hegemony*.

Howard (2006) argues that hegemony is when one social group rearranges a system in such a way that its dominance is seen as justifiable; in other words, it gains consent of dominance. In education, those in power who control education construct "official knowledge." This small, elite group constructs the knowledge that flows through schools in such a way as to disseminate the "truths" that perpetuate their own power. As Sonia Nieto and Patty Bode (2012) discuss in their book, *Affirming Diversity*, curriculum is contested political terrain, not neutral; it represents what is perceived to be consequential and necessary knowledge by those who are dominant in a society.

Nieto and Bode (2012) argue that knowledge taught in our schools reflects that which does not offend the dominant culture and is least controversial. In our schools, the textbooks in all subject areas exclude information from unpopular perspectives or the perspectives of the disempowered groups in our society. The supposed truths that are taught in schools give the impression that Whites are always correct in their decision making.

Howard (2006) describes this as the assumption of rightness. The assumption of rightness is the idea that Whites don't consider themselves as having culture; they just consider themselves to be right. It is an interesting notion that the "founding fathers" of American history claimed to create a new society built on freedom and equality; however, only White wealthy males were afforded these rights. It is important to recognize the institutional structures that support racism have a historical basis in the nation's founding. Scientific race theories were a way of explaining the inferiority of the Other.

Another dynamic of White dominance is the legacy of privilege. This is a privilege afforded to Whites based solely on skin color (McIntosh, 2008); it is invisible to Whites and is also unearned. One of the things that the legacy of privilege brings with it is the luxury of ignorance. Howard (2006) describes this luxury when he declares that Whites know very little about those whom they define as the Other. If you know very little, it is very easy to make your own truths, which perpetuate whatever you want to believe to sustain your social position in society. It then becomes easy to create a society that is unjust and inequitable.

The legacy of White privilege and the luxury of ignorance have resulted in what I term *unearned privilege*. What have Whites done to earn any special privilege above those of other Americans who have toiled and sacrificed for this country? In fact, if we turn the tables on those who have labored and died to make America a great nation, the Whites might fall out of the privileged designation.

Christine Sleeter (2008) describes White privilege within the context of unequal power relations, discussing how European peoples ascended to power by stealing land, resources, and even human beings and that this has resulted in Whites framing the culture and the identity of people of color. As a result, Whites have been able to construct their image of what it means to be American. The term *American* is a claim that the Anglo-Saxons are the "real Americans" or the "standard" Americans and the rest are foreigners. These special privileges remain intact in public schools where the school curricula, high-stakes testing, teacher expectations, tracking policies, and other variables continue to privilege White students.

These privileges are detailed by Sleeter and Grant (2009), who write, "In 2003, only about 72 percent of all recent African American high school graduates were employed compared to about 89 percent of White recent high school graduates and 83 percent White high school dropouts" (p. 8). These special advantages can be seen in nearly every segment of our nation, from employment and housing to education and health care. The assumption of rightness creates blindness for those in the dominant group that is largely a result of the luxury of ignorance.

Howard (2006) argues that those in the dominant group know very little about those whom they define as the Other. Thus, twenty-first-century school leaders will need to learn how to be antiracist educators. A perusal of school administrator course offerings reveals a dearth of courses that address multicultural education. This poses a serious problem in properly preparing school leaders to effectively implement multicultural education into the school philosophy so that it permeates everything that happens in the school.

Preparation programs for school leaders continue to be based on a scientific management approach that is rooted in a Eurocentered approach to leadership—an approach that produces school leaders who are antimulticultural education. Another major problem in the preparation of school leaders is that the majority of professors in school administrator preparation programs are far removed from the realities of the classroom. As a result, they may be detached from the realities that students and teachers experience in school, thus limiting their ability to offer insight on eradicating the tension between administrators, teachers, and students. Additionally, these former administrators may have been good systems people, never critiquing education. This makes it imperative for future school leaders to have some knowledge of critical pedagogy to help them truly become leaders working for the empowerment and uplift of the entire school.

CONCLUSION

Finally, there is a great need to incorporate the research and writings of scholars in the field of multicultural education into school administrator programs. I would not be surprised to find that most school leaders may not know the major educational theorists in multicultural education and critical pedagogy. Effectively preparing school leaders to address multicultural education would remedy these shortcomings. To truly make the necessary changes that will ensure all of America's students are afforded high-quality education, colleges of education will have to rethink how they prepare school leaders. Multicultural education is key!

REFLECTIVE STEPS FOR EDUCATIONAL LEADERS

1. Think about multicultural education from a sociopolitical context. This will move you to think about policies and other systemic issues that prevent all students from experiencing educational equity and equality.
2. Critique policies and practices that negatively impact historically underserved students by questioning data sets that report the high suspension and expulsion of African American males or the overrepresentation of this population in special education.
3. Develop a strategic plan of action to dismantle educational disparities at your school.
4. Revisit transformative Black leadership. This means exploring Black leaders who offered a critique of the social injustices at the risk of their personal safety.
5. Conduct your own research study on how educational policy is developed. Question who are the architects of these policies.
6. The following books will prove helpful in understanding the sociopolitical context of education as it relates to this chapter: Joel Spring's *The Politics of American Education* (2010) and Joe Kincheloe's *Critical Pedagogy Primer* (2008).

Chapter 1

DISCUSSION QUESTIONS

1. Based on what you have read in this chapter, why is multicultural education important for educational leaders?
2. How do you envision incorporating multicultural education as an educational leader?
3. Have you observed or experienced White privilege in educational settings?
4. What can be done to improve the educational experiences of historically underserved students?

REFERENCES

Banks, J. A. (2001). Multicultural education: Historical development, dimensions, and practice. In J. A. Banks & C. M. Banks (Eds.), *Handbook of research on multicultural education* (pp. 3–24). San Francisco: Jossey-Bass.

Banks, J. A. (2005). *Cultural diversity and education: Foundations, curriculum, and teaching* (5th ed.). New York: Allyn & Bacon.

Banks, J. A. (2014). *An introduction to multicultural education* (5th ed.). Boston: Pearson.

Bond, H.M. (1939). *Negro education in Alabama: A study in cotton and steel.* Washington, DC: The Associated Publishers.

Dewey, J. (1889). *School and society.* USA: Phi Delta Kappa.

Freire, P. (2000). *Pedagogy of the oppressed.* New York: Continuum.

Gabbard, D., & E. Ross. (Eds.). (2004). *Defending public schools: Education under the security state.* Westport, CT: Greenwood Publishing Group.

Howard, G. (2006). *We can't teach what we don't know: White teachers in multiracial schools* (2nd ed.). New York: Teachers College Press.

Jenkins, R. (2009). A historical analysis of Black education: The impact of desegregation on African Americans. In A. Pitre, E. Pitre, R. Ray, & T. Pitre (Eds.), *Educating African American students: Foundations, curriculum and experiences* (pp. 3–18). Lanham, MD: Rowman & Littlefield Education.

McIntosh, P. (2008). White privilege: Unpacking the invisible backpack. In J. Noel (Ed.), *Classic edition sources: Multicultural education* (2nd ed.). Boston: McGraw-Hill.

McLaren, P. (2015). *Life in schools: An introduction to critical pedagogy in the foundations of education* (6th ed.). Boulder, CO: Paradigm.

Nieto, S., & P. Bode. (2012). *Affirming diversity: The sociopolitical context of multicultural education* (6th ed.). Boston: Allyn & Bacon.

Oakes, J., & M. Lipton. (2007). *Teaching to change the world* (3rd ed.). Boston: McGraw-Hill.

Pitre, A. (2009). Series foreword. In A. Pitre, E. Pitre, R. Ray, & T. Pitre (Eds.), *Educating African American students: Foundations, curriculum, and experiences* (pp. v–xi). Lanham, MD: Rowman & Littlefield Education.

Sleeter, C. (2008). White racism. In J. Noel (Ed.), *Classic edition sources: Multicultural education* (2nd ed.). Boston: McGraw-Hill.

Sleeter, C., & C. Grant. (2009). *Making choices for multicultural education: Five approaches to race, class, and gender* (6th ed.). Hoboken, NJ: John Wiley & Sons, Inc.

Suitts, S. (2010). *A new diverse majority: Students of color in the South's public schools.* Atlanta, GA: Southern Education Foundation.

Watkins, W. (2001). *The White architects of Black education: Ideology and power in America 1865–1954.* New York: Teachers College Press.

Wesley, C.H. (1935). *Richard Allen: Apostle of freedom.* Washington, DC: The Associated Publishers.

Woodson, C. G. (1919, 1968). *The education of the negro prior to 1861* New York: Arno Press.

Woodson, C. G. (2008). *The mis-education of the Negro*. Drewryville, VA: Kha Books.
Yen, H. (2009). *White Americans' majority to end by mid-century*. Associated Press, December 16.

Chapter Two

School Leaders and Multicultural Education in Black Schools

A Critical Race Theory–Antiracist Perspective

Abul Pitre and Pamela Adams

INTRODUCTION

Scholars studying educational leadership have noted that establishing a positive school culture is essential to the enhancement of school performance (Sergiovanni, 1999; Deal & Peterson, 2009). Deal and Peterson (2009), in describing a Navajo school that experienced high levels of failure, noted that when the school leadership began to align the school culture around Navajo history and cultural experiences the achievement levels of Navajo students improved drastically. The success for Navajo students went beyond academic achievement to the point that students and teachers became a community. Thus, they were a part of a communal spirit that evoked deep personal commitments to one another.

In a study on Black history, Pitre (2011a) noticed the powerful impact that a Black history course and program had on transforming a predominately Black school bereft with gang violence, low test scores, and student apathy. The students in Pitre's study were able to transform themselves as well as their school because they were empowered by learning Black history from a critical perspective, which in turn resulted in the students taking action against unjust school policies and racist educators. What emerged from these powerful experiences was a new culture whereby students who were once apathetic and hostile toward each other were now aware of how the oppressor consciousness had impacted their thinking toward one another.

Freire (2000) describes the struggle these students encountered: "They are at one and the same time themselves and the oppressor whose consciousness they have internalized" (p. 48). By gaining knowledge of self, the students became conscious of the source of their oppression and were able to turn against their domestication, resulting in unity among the students. More importantly, the critical study of Black history resulted in students being motivated to learn, thus changing the culture of the school.

It is well known that incorporating multicultural education in schools can create school communities where students are empowered and energized about learning. One of the misnomers that have impacted multicultural education is that too often educators see it as the sharing of cultural artifacts among diverse groups. What emerges from this kind of thinking is a very shallow understanding of multicultural education. To really get at the heart of multicultural education, school leaders will need to move beyond simplistic views of multicultural education to one that addresses the systemic inequality that exists in schools.

On too many occasions when speaking with educators in predominantly Black schools, they argue that the students need to be exposed to more cultures. Yet these same educators rarely realize that Black students have a very limited knowledge of themselves. In an apparent misunderstanding of multicultural education, Black history is described as antimulticultural. Apparently, these educators have lost sight of the role that Black scholars initiating Black history played in forming the foundation of multicultural education.

James Banks, one of the leading multicultural education scholars in the 1970s, had a specific focus on teaching Black history in public schools. He wrote, "The goal of Black history should be to help students develop the ability to make reflective decisions so that they can resolve personal problems and through social action influence public policy and develop a sense of political efficacy" (Banks, 1973, p. 152). Neither Banks nor his contemporaries envisioned the teaching of Black history as the regurgitation of names and dates of Black people who were accepted by the dominant group.

Black history was seen as a powerful force that could liberate Black students from the oppressive conditions in which they lived, creating in them the ability to solve problems such as "poverty, political powerlessness, low self-esteem, consumer exploitation, institutional racism, and political alienation" (Banks, 1973, p. 152). In some southern states where Black students are now the majority in public schools, there are high levels of poverty.

The Southern Education Foundation reported in 2006 that the population of low-income students in Louisiana's public schools was 84 percent; in Mississippi, low-income students accounted for 75 percent of the public school student population (Suitts, 2007). Banks eloquently describes the kind of education these students should receive: "We must radicalize Black and other colonized students so that they will continually challenge the position of those in power. We should also train them so that they will develop the skills and knowledge to obtain power and use it to build institutions they will control" (p. 152).

Proper education of students in majority Black and low-income schools will require educators, particularly school leaders, to have knowledge about critical theories of education. Today more than ever, predominately Black schools need multicultural education. The multicultural education that we describe in this chapter goes beyond the cultural elements of diverse groups of students to the systemic issues that plague predominately Black schools.

This chapter incorporates the theoretical frameworks found in critical race theory of education and antiracist education described by Nieto and Bode (2012) in their sociopolitical perspective of multicultural education. Moving away from the human relations approach and the additive approach to multicultural education, we discuss racism, critical race theory, and antiracist education in relation to predominately Black schools.

What emerges is a review of the school curriculum, school policies such as tracking, teacher perceptions of Black students, a discussion of critical pedagogy, and social justice issues in education. The chapter gives leaders in predominantly Black schools a perspective of multicultural education that "challenges and rejects racism and other forms of discrimination in schools and society" (Nieto & Bode, 2012, p. 42).

RACISM

Racism is a deeply rooted phenomenon in American life that has deep historical ties to education. American education will reveal that the education of Black people has been a major concern for the ruling elite. Prior to the Civil War when the first Blacks were brought to the Americas to be made slaves, an education plan was formulated that would strip the newly arrived peoples of their culture.

Immediately following the Civil War, wealthy philanthropists crafted an educational agenda that would allow them to maintain control over Black people. Imbedded in their agenda was the use of race as an ideological weapon to relegate Blacks to second-class citizenship. Watkins (2001) posits, "Colonial education had to be fitted to the American South. This undertaking required the efforts of both the ideologists and the financiers. Corporate philanthropists joined forces with racial sociologists to design seventy-five years of education for Blacks" (p. 42).

The education that Blacks were to receive was rooted in White supremacy, ultimately designed to make Black people White supremacists in the sense that Blacks would be educated to see Whites as the superior people, thus making them more subservient, docile, and obedient. Watkins (2001) describes this "special kind of education" for southern Blacks as one that "attempted to reconcile Negro subservience with the new arrangements of power, diffuse potential turmoil, and pacify diverse elements" (p. 42). Woodson (2008) called this kind of education *mis-education*, and decried,

> The Negro's mind has been brought under the control of his oppressors. The problem of holding the Negro down, therefore, is easily solved. When you control a man's thinking you don't have to tell him to stand here or go yonder. He will find his "proper place" and will stay in it. You do not need to send him to the back door. He will go without being told. In fact, if there is no back door, he will cut one for his special benefit. His education makes it necessary. (p. xiii)

The historical record of American education illuminates the role of racism and its relationship to Black education. The systemic racism that forms the foundation of American education is one of the areas that some school leaders are afraid to address. Part of the problem in not confronting racism by school leaders may lie in the fact that a majority are under the power of school boards that are largely made up of Whites.

Blount (1994) characterizes this relationship thus: "Administrators are appointed by the persons to whom they must later account. Essentially, administrators tend to serve as functionaries whose roles are carefully defined, their hierarchical positions fixed" (p. 58). She goes on to acknowledge that "school board members have tended to choose people most like themselves: White males amenable to the needs of the affluent and influential members of the community" (p. 56). Blount's analysis could mean that school administrators are selected based on their willingness to accept racist and classist institutional structures.

In cases where school leaders have an antiracist philosophy, they may be caught in the dilemma of facing majority White school boards and White teaching staffs that have a White supremacist worldview. Under this kind of environment, antiracist school leaders may find themselves handcuffed when it comes to addressing issues of racism in a way that it brings about systemic changes. Some school leaders may not even be cognizant that racism exists and in fact may become alarmed or feel guilty when the topic of racism is brought up. In fact, a school leader's job may depend on how well he or she can avoid tackling the dynamics of racism.

Despite the lack of discourse or acknowledgement of racism in schools, the media has played a major role in depicting Black youth as being savage and bestial, and the result is that in predominately Black schools, school leaders may believe Black students to be culturally deprived. The cultural deprivation theory purports that the reason students may not do well in school is because their environment and the individual cultural experiences they receive from home are antithetical to education. School leaders working from this paradigm will more than likely support policies that result in more punitive school policies toward Black students.

Another possible consequence of believing that Black students are culturally deprived is described by Freire (2000) in *Pedagogy of the Oppressed*: "If others do not have more, it is because they are incompetent and lazy, and worst of all is their unjustifiable ingratitude towards the generous gestures of the dominant class. Precisely because they are ungrateful and envious, the oppressed are regarded as potential enemies who must be watched" (p. 59). This kind of thinking results in school policies whereby children in preK–sixth grade are graded on everything from class work to walking to the restroom. The environment is one that requires monitoring the child's every movement, which in turn makes school unnatural and drives large numbers of Black youth from the innate pursuit of knowledge.

Racist teachers and school leaders may also seek severe punishment for Black youth who seem to deviate from the domestication imposed by schools. Zero-tolerance policies are used as a way to suspend and expel Black youth for what may be minor violations. Reyes (2006) contends that ineffective, zero-tolerance policies result in large numbers of minority students being removed from schools. According to data retrieved from the National Center for Educational Statistics, in 2002 minority students were disproportionately suspended and given more severe punishments.

School leaders must be mindful of how their thinking about Black youth may perpetuate the racism that exists in the larger society; Nieto and Bode (2012) write, "As institutions, schools respond to and reflect the larger society. Therefore, it is not surprising that racism finds its way into schools in much the same way that it finds its way into other institutions, such as housing, employment, and the criminal justice system" (p. 66). A major element for school leaders to include in the implementation of multicultural education in Black schools is antiracist education and professional development for the faculty and staff; administrators should be the first to go through such training.

A major characteristic of multicultural education as described by some multicultural scholars is that it is antiracist. Nieto and Bode (2012) contend that "antiracism, indeed antidiscrimination in general, is at the very core of a multicultural perspective. It is essential to keep the antiracist nature of multicultural education in mind because, in many schools, even some that espouse a multicultural philosophy, only superficial aspects of multicultural education are apparent" (p. 43).

Rather, they argue that often racism works itself insidiously into schools: "Racism is also manifested in rigid ability tracking, low expectations of students based on their identity, and inequitably funded schools, among other policies" (p. 66). Thus, school leaders need to be educated to become antiracist leaders that in turn could create the powerful changes that are needed to ensure that all children have an opportunity for equal education. Instead of avoiding the reality of racism, school leaders could perhaps be guided by the concepts found in critical race theory.

CRITICAL RACE THEORY IN EDUCATION

Critical race theory began with law scholars who were upset with the slow pace of change needed to ensure equal rights for those who were marginalized and disenfranchised. Harvard law professors, most notably Derrick Bell and Alan Freeman, coined the term *critical race theory* by arguing that racism permeates every aspect of American life. Bell and Freeman's analysis of racism was later applied by Ladson-Billings and Tate (1995) to describe racism in education; thus, critical race theory in education was birthed into existence.

In describing critical race theory, Taylor (2009) writes, "The first observation is that racism is a normal fact of daily life in the U.S. society that is neither aberrant nor rare. The assumptions of White superiority are so ingrained in political, legal, and educational structures that they are almost unrecognizable" (p. 4). When Lipman (1998) describes the disproportionate number of Black children in special education behavior disorder classes or with high numbers of suspension and expulsion, one has to look at the deeper reasons for such. Perhaps on the surface these issues depict a problem with Black children; however, these issues may also be illuminating a much bigger phenomenon that is rooted in racism. Not only are some school policies reflecting elements of racial inequalities but also areas such as the curriculum are imbued with racism.

Unbeknown to some school leaders, imbedded in the curriculum is a covert form of racism. Ladson-Billings (2009) argues that "critical race theory sees the official school curriculum as a culturally specific artifact designed to maintain a White supremacist master script," meaning "the stories of African Americans are muted and erased when they challenge dominant culture authority and power" (p. 29). Nowhere is this more forcefully seen than in the examples of Marcus Garvey, Carter G. Woodson, Elijah Muhammad, Malcolm X, and Louis Farrakhan—Black leaders with philosophical viewpoints that were incongruent with the world's most powerful and elite. In maintaining the hierarchical structures, school leaders may unknowingly believe the official curriculum is really about educating Black and other marginalized youth. Black students who resist the racist school curriculum through any number of ways, including challenging the teacher, are often seen as troublemakers.

School leaders very seldom approach high-stakes testing from the perspective that it is the right arm of White supremacist thinking (Pitre, 2009). In an effort to ensure that end-of-grade scores are maintained (because lower test scores may result in the unemployment of school leaders and teachers), school leaders are forced to spend a considerable amount of time making sure the school community accepts and works to raise test scores. While one cannot argue with school leaders for addressing the so-called testing problem, they are ultimately being led by a necessary illusion that portrays them to students as an oppressor when in fact school leaders are only overseeing the policies and rules dictated from on high. Under these circumstances it becomes important for school leaders to study how critical race theorists see testing as a ploy to ensure White supremacy:

> For critical race theorists, intelligence testing has been a movement to legitimize African American student deficiency under the guise of scientific rationalism. If the working-class white is "achieving" at a higher level than Blacks, then they feel relatively superior. This allows Whites with real power to exploit both poor Whites and Blacks. Throughout U.S. history, the subordination of Blacks has been built on "scientific" theories (e.g., intelligence testing) that depend on racial stereotypes about Blacks that make their condition appear appropriate. (Ladson-Billings, 2009, p. 30)

A good working knowledge of critical race theory might help school leaders address what is called the *cultural difference theory*, which argues that the problem is not children's home backgrounds but the way schools operate that causes disproportionate poor performance among historically marginalized groups. Additionally, school leaders studying critical race theory would be able to develop insights about how to address the testing frenzy so that Black children would become conscious of this master scripting and consequently take up the challenge of overcoming the White supremacist assessment models designed to relegate them to a form of second-class citizenship.

In the classroom, school leaders would support teachers who empower students to examine critical issues such as racism and its impact on their daily lives. When talking with teachers, one of the things that they highlight is that school leaders do not welcome classroom conversation not rooted in the dominant discourse. These teachers are often threatened with punishment for engaging students in dialogue that reveals how historical injustices have impacted contemporary society.

For instance, some school leaders would reject a discussion of the movie *Panther* along with a critique of how drugs have made their way into the Black community. The historical examination of lynching, murder, and powerful Black figures would certainly lead to a teacher being reprimanded or fired (Pitre, 2011a).

Only safe figures or those that fit the constructs of the dominant society are presented to Black students. Perhaps one of the reasons school leaders are afraid of teachers engaging students in conversations about racism is that these conversations could reveal the covert racism that exists in schools and lead Black students to protest against it. Discourse on racism would also expose racist educators and policies, possibly leading to students working collectively to disrupt the inhumane and racist treatment they experience in school.

Another area in which scholars have noticed racial disparities are in rigid ability tracking, which some contend is usually race and class based (Nieto & Bode, 2012; Oakes & Lipton, 2007). In too many cases students of color are relegated to the lower tracks while White students are put into higher tracks—a phenomenon Spring (2006) labels second-generation segregation. One should not be surprised to visit a school assembly for honor students and find that even in schools that are majority Black, White students will in some cases make up the majority of students with higher grade point averages.

In predominately Black schools with gifted and talented programs, White students again may make up the majority of the students in such programs. However, when it comes to special education behavior disorder, Black students, particularly Black males, may make up the majority of students in the program (Pitre & Lewis, 2009). The disproportionate numbers of Black males in special education behavior disorder programs is coupled with a larger problem of how students in these special settings are treated.

In a study on the experience of Black boys in special education, Pitre (2011b) found that the students surveyed felt that teachers didn't care about them. The students in Pitre's study reported learning how to sleep while sitting straight up in class; in other words, they learned how to pretend they were learning. They talked at length about how their school experiences made them feel worthless and reported they had been tricked into special education by racist educators who devalued them. One has to wonder if school leaders are even cognizant of the social injustices propagated against Black students on a daily basis.

A major part of the problem in Black schools also deals with the teaching force. According to some scholars, teachers in low-income majority Black schools are often those with the least credentials. Additionally, it is well known that the majority of public school teachers in the United States are White, middle-class females. And while the problem may not necessarily be skin color, Kunjufu (2002) and Sleeter (2004) offer two perspectives on the issue of White teachers.

Kunjufu (2002) contends that while the race of teachers may be critical, "I believe that the most important factor impacting the academic achievement of African American children is not the race or gender of the teacher but the teacher's expectations" (p. 17). Sleeter (2004) counters that "teacher race does matter, and for reasons that include and extend beyond issues of cultural congruence in the classroom . . . a predominantly White teaching force in a racist and multicultural society is not good for anyone, if we wish to have schools reverse rather than produce racism" (p. 163).

School leaders faced with a majority White teaching staff and predominately Black student population are placed in a precarious situation whereby some White teachers will profess a color-blind perspective when in reality they are trying not to implicate themselves as being racist. Sleeter explains, "People do not deny seeing what they actually do not see. Rather, they profess to be colorblind when trying to suppress negative images they attach to people of color, given the significance of color in the United States, the dominant ideology of equal opportunity, and the relationship between race and observable measures of success" (p. 169).

In subtle or sometimes more overt ways, White teachers may discourage Black students in the classroom. For example, on a visit to an elementary class composed of majority Black students, it was observed that when asking questions about a previous assignment, the White teacher more often called on the White students. The teacher ignored Black students who raised their hands to respond to nearly every question.

Nieto and Bode (2012), citing the McDermott study, point out that "the Black children had to try three times harder to catch the teacher's eye for signs of approval, affection, and encouragement" (p. 71). Scenarios such as this may explain some possible reasons that Black children are not doing well on standardized testing as compared with White students. Students who experience this kind of treatment may lose interest in school and put forth less effort because teachers devalue them.

Regarding the role that White teachers play in the dehumanization of Black children, Sleeter (2004) suggests it occurs because White teachers may be "fearful that well-educated African American, Latino, and Native American students might launch a bold critique of White institutions and White people, and aware that parity in achievement across groups would threaten a major advantage to White people that their children currently enjoy" (p. 171).

Another possible reason that may explain why some White teachers ignore Black children may be a result of dysconscious racism, a term King (1991) coined to describe the "uncritical habit of mind (including perceptions, attitudes, assumptions, and beliefs) that justifies inequity and exploitation by accepting the existing order of things as given" (p. 135). The uncritical habit of mind could mean that some White teachers are not really conscious of their racism.

A good example of dysconscious racism is a third-grade teacher who has students reading biographies for a social studies class. Of the fifteen students in the class, ten are Black and five are White; yet the teacher has not assigned a single Black figure for students to read. The assignment has been ongoing since September, and it is now late January. Some of the Black students have begun to question why they have not been assigned biographies of a Black person. The teacher in this example is reinforcing a White supremacist perspective by not showing the Black students any positive images depicting Black people as world shapers. Conversely, the White students, despite being in the minority, have been reinforced to think they have accomplished more than other groups.

Woodson (2008) wrote that "the same educational process which inspires and stimulates the oppressor with the thought that he is everything and has accomplished everything worthwhile depresses and crushes the spark of genius in the Negro by making him feel that his race does not amount to much and never will measure up to the standards of other peoples" (p. xiii). This is the sad reality that too many Black students experience in school. However, school leaders working from a multicultural and critical race theory perspective would be able to address the racism that exists in a variety of ways within the school.

CRITICAL PEDAGOGY FOR SCHOOL LEADERS

School leaders working in predominately Black schools are in dire need of knowledge in critical pedagogy or critical educational theory. Critical pedagogy, also described as liberation pedagogy, has a strong tradition in the experiences of Black people. W. E. B. Du Bois, Carter G. Woodson, Elijah Muhammad, and others offered the quintessential grounding of the tenets espoused in critical pedagogy.

Contemporaries of these great leaders are Afrocentric scholars who have continued to challenge oppressive school structures for Black students. Pitre (2011a) has merged the ideas found in Afrocentric education with multicultural education and critical pedagogy to form what is termed *critical Black pedagogy in education*, an examination of Black leaders, ministers, and teachers and their ideas about Black education. Banks (2014) notes that Afrocentric education is multicultural education because it does not profess to be the only perspective for students but instead offers the African and African American viewpoints. Scholars in the Afrocentric paradigm and critical pedagogues are concerned with questions like: Who decides what the educational agenda should entail? Why are some bodies of knowledge included in the curriculum while others are excluded?

Historically, those in powerful positions manipulate the education of Black people to maintain control over them. W. E. B. Du Bois, in critiquing industrial schooling as it related to the role of Black colleges, wrote, "It is not then in its method but in its practical objects that the Negro college has failed. It is in handling on knowledge and experience but what knowledge and for what end" (Aptheker, 1973, p. 69). Du Bois was not alone in his critique of Black education; Carter G. Woodson started a revolutionary movement by pointing out the necessity of Black history for Black people.

Woodson offered a powerful historical truth when he wrote, "The so-called modern education, with all its defects, however, does others so much more because it has been worked out in conformity to the needs of those who have enslaved and oppressed weaker peoples" (p. xii). Further, he spoke to the power relations that critical pedagogy addresses:

> Negroes have no control over their education [and] have little voice in their other affairs pertaining thereto. In a few cases Negroes have been chosen as members of the public boards of education, and some have been appointed members of private boards, but these Negroes are always such a small minority that they do not figure in the final working of the educational program. The education of the Negroes, then, the most important thing in the uplift of the Negroes, is almost entirely in the hands of those who have enslaved them and now segregate them. (p. 22)

Woodson's scathing critique of Black education offers much insight for today's school leaders. Schools that serve large numbers of Black children are still under the control of Whites in power.

Industrial education has been sidelined to fit the technological world in which we now live. Schools today give the appearance that they are designed to truly educate Black students when in fact the outcome of schooling leaves Black people as a group too dependent on others.

Elijah Muhammad saw this as a problem and argued that Black people needed to develop their own institutions; education would then serve as a way to empower Black people to get something of their own. He urged Blacks to "get an education, but one which will instill the idea and desire to get something of your own, a country of your own, and jobs of your own" (1965, p. 40). He argued that the education of Black students had only resulted in them "adding to the storehouse of their teacher," meaning their education served the interest of those ruling the society.

He vehemently opposed the type of schooling that Black people were receiving, and he exposed the power relationship in plain terms so that the most unlearned could grasp the reality of what was taking place: "Today with all of our White civilized schooling, we have not been taught our own. They will never teach us of our own . . . The slave master will not teach you the knowledge of self, as there would not be a master-slave relationship" (pp. 48, 37).

The slave-master relationship can be found in the way schools reproduce what exists in the larger society. Bowles (2008 cited in Noel) observed what has been termed *social reproduction theory*, which contends that schools operate within a capitalist society and thus, unequal schooling is a result of "class distinctions created by capitalism" (p. 20). Anyon (2006) revisited an earlier study to identify four types of schools—working-class, middle-class, affluent-class, and executive-elite schools. She observed that the curriculum and how children experienced the curriculum was quite different depending on the type of school they attended. For example, in the working-class schools, students were expected to memorize and regurgitate information; the executive-elite school, however, allowed students to engage the subjects more creatively, helping these students to create knowledge.

All of the schools in Anyon's study were majority White, which has significant implications for predominately Black schools. What does the social reproduction theory suggest for Black students who have historically been educated to serve Whites? Elijah Muhammad (1965) asserted,

> Since our being brought in chains to the shores of America, our brain power, labor, skills, talent, and wealth have been taken, given, and spent toward building and adding to the civilization of another people . . . We must stop the process of giving our brain power, labor, and wealth to our slave-masters' children. We must eliminate the master-slave relationship. (pp. 56–57)

Like many scholars who study the social reproduction theory, Muhammad was saying that Black people have been educated in a way that benefits others.

Critical pedagogues in education contend that the curriculum is designed to enforce or enhance the race and class inequalities in the society. Apple (2004) succinctly describes the historical role of curriculum in maintaining inequalities: "This view of unequal distribution of responsibility and power was reflected when they talked about how curriculum differentiation would fulfill two social purposes—education for leadership and education for what they called 'followership'" (p. 72).

School leaders working to transform predominately Black schools need to have a good understanding of how schools are continuing a long historical tradition that has served the best interest of the ruling elite. Perhaps this explains Apple's (2004) contention that schools are working fine because they are doing exactly what they were designed to do—leave large numbers of children behind.

In keeping Black students subjugated, the architects of modern Black education have put together what Apple calls "official knowledge"—knowledge that the state sanctions and approves for students to learn. Students that realize they are being domesticated and some cases dehumanized resist school; because they have not been taught how to organize to voice their discontent with the schooling process, they begin to act out in ways that cast them as troublemakers.

In some cases the oppression that occurs with Black males may result in them taking out their frustration on other Black male students. Freire provides some insight on Black on Black violence in schools with the claim that the oppressed have internalized the oppressor's consciousness. As a result of internalizing the oppressor's view of themselves, the oppressed begin to take out their frustration on their fellows.

In summary, school leaders grounded in the tenets of critical pedagogy may be more inclined to struggle with Black students creating a consciousness that truly empowers the entire school community. What might evolve from this is a totally different school culture—one where Black students are part of a communal spirit, the same kind of spirit that allowed them to survive the cruelties of racism in America.

CONCLUSION

What, then, is the role of school leaders in a process of systemic change? That is the crux of the problem. The truth is that in order to understand and change the focus of schools, its leaders will need to become social justice advocates. As social justice advocates, school leaders will truly become leaders, guiding students, teachers, and their community to a much greater meaning for the purpose of education. Multicultural education could potentially transform predominately Black schools by helping students to gain knowledge that will empower them to solve the problems that impact their communities.

For multicultural education to be successful in Black schools, leaders will need to abandon the belief that multicultural education is about the sharing of foods and artifacts from diverse cultures. Multicultural education for educational leaders should provide these leaders with profound insights on how to dismantle the racist and oppressive school structures that deny Black students the right to a quality education.

Multicultural education must permeate the entire school environment in order to bring about the substantive change that will benefit disenfranchised youth in predominately Black schools. Leaders must take into account that any change should be sequential and carefully thought out with regard to the community and the students. The steps that follow could benefit school leaders to this end.

REFLECTIVE STEPS FOR EDUCATIONAL LEADERS

1. Develop a personal multicultural education library and commit to reading literature related to multicultural education.

2. Study the work and life of great Black leaders. This will offer much insight about how to really become a leader. For some school leaders, studying Black leaders will be the first time they have departed from the Eurocentered school leadership programs that focus solely on the ideas of White educators.

3. Join organizations such as the National Association for Multicultural Education, the National Council for Black Education, the National Association for Black Education, and the Association for the Study of African American Life and History. These organizations will allow the school leader to gain more knowledge of educational issues related to Black education and provide opportunities to network with people who have similar interests. Networking will be important for school leaders who take an emancipatory approach to the education of Black youth. In some cases these leaders may find themselves marginalized by the majority of school leaders.

4. School leaders must envision their work as a prophetic calling or mission. Purpel and McLaurin (2004) highlight the significance of educators in seeing their work as a much higher calling—one that addresses the moral and spiritual crisis in education.

SUGGESTIONS FOR THE SCHOOL

1. Create an on-campus multicultural education library for faculty and staff.
2. Recruit more Black teachers, particularly Black males who are conscious and willing to work for the uplift of Black students.
3. Motivate faculty and staff to start a reading club whereby they read one book a semester related to the education of Black students.
4. Hold small group roundtable discussions with teachers in their respective teaching departments.
5. Invite guest speakers and provide multicultural education workshops once teachers have gained some knowledge of multicultural education. What happens in some cases is that school leaders provide workshops in multicultural education but the teachers are unprepared for critical conversations that will lead them to examine their perceptions of Black students and their education.
6. Develop a relationship with the community to include churches, civic organizations, and community leaders.
7. Create open lines of communication with parents and empower them to take ownership in the school.
8. Take small steps with diverse groups of faculty, staff, and students. Benchmark change and advocate for the success of students.

9. Review school policies such as tracking, zero tolerance, and special education placement, and work to dismantle the disproportionate number of Black students being placed in lower tracks. Address the small number of Black students in gifted and talented programs.
10. Incorporate a critical Black history program that makes students conscious of social injustices. The program should be a culminating project that empowers Black youth to address the problems in their communities. Invite people to participate who are willing to speak truth to power.
11. Engage Black youth in a way that they are empowered to take control of their lives. The cultural deficit model should not be used as an excuse when it comes to educating Black students.
12. Develop small group sessions with the students to discuss issues that are important to them.
13. Establish a student government association that is not teacher or school leader driven. Allow the students to select their leaders to represent their interest to teachers and school leaders. Changing the oppressive schooling experiences of Black students in predominately Black schools will not be an easy task. It will take courageous leaders who are willing to challenge the status quo to ensure equality of education.

DISCUSSION QUESTIONS

1. Why is developing a culture that is congruent with students' cultural experiences important?
2. How do you envision building a culturally responsive school community for diverse students?
3. What does it mean to be an antiracist educational leader?
4. Can you identify policies and practices at your school that may be oppressive?
5. How can educational leaders disrupt policies that oppress students?
6. What are your thoughts about critical pedagogy and critical educational theory?
7. What do you think educational leaders can learn from the study of African American leaders?

REFERENCES

Anyon, J. (2006). Social class, school knowledge, and the hidden curriculum: Retheorizing reproduction. In L. Weis, C. McCarthy, & G. Dimitriadis (Eds.), *Ideology, curriculum, and the new sociology of education* (pp. 37–46). New York: Taylor and Francis Group.
Apple, M. (2004). *Ideology and curriculum* (3rd ed.). New York: Routledge.

Banks, J. A. (Ed.). (1973). *Teaching ethnic studies: Concepts and strategies.* Washington, DC: National Council for the Social Studies.

Banks, J. A. (2014). *An introduction to multicultural education* (5th ed.). Boston: Pearson.

Blount, T. (1994). One postmodern feminist perspective on educational leadership: And aren't I a leader? In S. Maxcy (Ed.), *Postmodern school leadership: Meeting the crisis in educational administration* (pp. 47–60). Praeger Publishers.

Bowles, S. (2008). Unequal education and the reproduction of the social division of labor. In J. Noel (Ed.), *Sources in multicultural education* (pp. 20–23). New York: McGraw-Hill.

Deal, T., & K. Peterson. (2009). *Shaping school culture: Pitfalls, paradoxes, and promises* (2nd ed.). San Francisco: Jossey-Bass.

Du Bois, W. E. B., & H. Aptheker (Eds.) (1973). *The education of Black people: Ten critiques, 1906–1960.* Boston: University of Massachusetts Press.

Freire, P. (2000). *Pedagogy of the oppressed.* New York: Continuum.

Jenkins, R. (2009). A historical analysis of Black education: The impact of desegregation on African Americans. In A. Pitre et al. (Eds.), *Educating African American students: Foundations, curriculum, and experiences* (pp. 3–18). Lanham, MD: Rowman & Littlefield Education.

King, J. (1991). Dysconscious racism: Ideology, identity, and the miseducation of teachers. *Journal of Negro Education* 60, no. 2: 133–46.

Kunjufu, J. (2002). *Black students, middle class teachers.* Chicago, IL: African American Images.

Ladson-Billings, G. (2009). Just what is critical race theory and what's it doing in a nice field like education? In E. Taylor, D. Gillborn, & G. Ladson-Billings (Eds.), *Foundations of critical race theory in education* (pp. 17–36). New York: Routledge.

Ladson-Billings, G., & W. Tate. (1995). Toward a critical race theory of education. *Teachers College Record* 97, no. 1: 47–68.

Lipman, P. (1998). *Race, class, and power in school restructuring.* New York: SUNY Press.

Muhammad, E. (1965). *Message to the Blackman in America.* Chicago, IL: Final Call.

Nieto, S., & P. Bode. (2008). *Affirming diversity: The sociopolitical context of multicultural education* (5th ed.). Boston: Pearson.

Nieto, S., & P. Bode. (2012). *Affirming diversity: The sociopolitical context of multicultural education* (6th ed.). Boston: Pearson.

Oakes, J., & M. Lipton. (2007). *Teaching to change the world* (3rd ed.). Boston: McGraw-Hill.

Pitre, A. (2009). Series foreword. In A. Pitre, E. Pitre, R. Ray, & T. Pitre (Eds.), *Educating African American students: Foundations, curriculum, and experiences* (pp. v–xi). Lanham, MD: Rowman & Littlefield Education.

Pitre, A. (2011a). *Freedom fighters: Struggles instituting the study of Black history in K–12 education.* San Francisco, CA: Cognella Academic Publishers.

Pitre, E. (2011b). *Locked in: African American males in special education.* New York: Linus Publications.

Pitre, E., & C. Lewis. (2009). The experiences of African American males in special education: An analysis of the student perspective. In A. Pitre, E. Pitre, R. Ray, & T. Pitre (Eds.), *Educating African American students: Foundations, curriculum, and experiences* (pp. 107–24). Lanham, MD: Rowman & Littlefield Education.

Purpel, D., & W. McLaurin. (2004). *Reflections on the moral and spiritual crisis in education.* Westport, CT: Bergin & Garvey.

Reyes, A. (2006). *Discipline, achievement, race: Is zero tolerance the answer?* Lanham, MD: Rowman & Littlefield Education.

Sergiovanni, T. (1999). *The lifeworld of leadership: Creating culture, community, and personal meaning in our schools.* San Francisco, CA: Jossey-Bass.

Sleeter, C. (1994). White racism. *Multicultural Education* 1, no. 4: 5–8, 39.

Sleeter, C. (2004). How White teachers construct race. In G. Ladson Billings & D. Gillborn (Eds.), *The RoutledgeFalmer reader in multicultural education* (pp. 163–78). London and New York: RoutledgeFalmer.

Spring, J. (2006). *American education.* New York: McGraw-Hill.

Suitts, S. (2007). *A new majority: Low income students in the South's public schools*. Atlanta, GA: Southern Education Foundation.

Taylor, E. (2009). The foundations of critical race theory in education: An introduction. In E. Taylor, D. Gillborn, & G. Ladson-Billings (Eds.), *Foundations of critical race theory in education* (pp. 1–16). New York: Routledge.

Watkins, W. (2001). *The White architects of Black education: Ideology and power in America 1865–1954*. New York: Teachers College Press.

Woodson, C. G. (2008). *The mis-education of the Negro*. Drewryville, VA: Kha Books.

Chapter Three

The Cultural Awakening of a White Educator

We Can't Lead Students We Don't Know

Mindy Vickers

INTRODUCTION

In his groundbreaking book, *We Can't Teach What We Don't Know: White Teachers, Multiracial Schools*, Gary Howard (2006) describes the cultural blindness that White educators often bring to the teaching profession. Howard's text, while specifically addressing White teachers, offers much insight for White educational leaders. Young and Laible (2000) also highlight the need for White educational leaders to be engaged in the antiracist perspectives of multicultural education. Educational leaders are faced each year with students that come from various races, social classes, religious backgrounds, and learning styles. The diverse student populations in public schools essentially mean that school leaders must grasp concepts in multicultural education; how else can they expect to lead students they don't know?

This chapter draws on Howard's (2006) work to examine the experiences of a White educator with virtually no experience or knowledge of multicultural education. It particularly examines the stages of White identity using Howard's descriptions of Helm's work on identity formation. This chapter chronicles the evolution of a White educator's experiences in a doctoral program that caused her to critically reflect on the concept of Whiteness and what it means to be a White educator.

45

EVOLUTION OF A WHITE EDUCATOR

The White educator described in this chapter grappled with the color-blind concept. At times she believed that she had to treat kids differently based on their cultural backgrounds and at other times she sought to treat all kids the same. The process of addressing the cultural dynamics that occur in schools has been an evolving process for this educator who has worked in public education for fifteen years as a teacher and administrator. It has transformed her and the way she sees her responsibilities toward the children in her school, and it is far from over.

Looking back to her childhood, she doesn't remember much about school before third grade. Although she attended public school in Georgia for three years, she has no idea about the racial makeup of the school. When she was a third-grader, her family moved to a small town in the Midwest. She doesn't remember any non-White students until high school, and even then, she only remembers there being two non-White students who were the children of a Filipino doctor in town. She knows there were no non-White teachers, administrators, custodians, cafeteria workers, or secretaries employed by the school district during her entire tenure until her graduation in 1988. She doesn't know if this is still the case, but she knows the district's student population is beginning to be more diverse.

She considers herself intelligent and was a good student. Being exceptional with numbers, her abilities in English and humanities courses were lacking in terms of paying attention to detail and analyzing or interpreting things. That being said, she does not remember any time during class where she talked about, read, researched, or was presented information by anyone other than White authors or information that came straight out of the textbooks. She has no doubt that they talked about African Americans and slavery in history class, but she is relatively sure it was from the perspective of the textbook, and she thinks because they were all White it was covered quickly.

She has no recollection of anything like a Black history program or a multicultural celebration or assembly. She's quite sure she had no idea there was a Black History Month until she moved to the Southeast in 1994 after graduating from college. She also has no real recollection of any discussions about people of other races. She was friends with a younger Filipino student who was friends with one of her neighbors, and they all hung out and went places together. Yet she never remembers any discussion about his culture. She saw him as just "one of the gang." She didn't treat him any differently than she treated her other friends.

It was only when they drove forty-five minutes to the mall in a nearby "big city" did she see people who were non-White. She was a cheerleader, a volleyball player, and she ran track, and in the majority of her athletic contests, all the players on the teams involved were White as well. If they drove an hour south to a large metropolitan area with an airport, it was one of the few encounters she had with non-Whites, but those interactions were short and of no substance. Howard (2006) describes her dilemma when he talks about the luxury of ignorance. Her limited interaction with non-Whites was not because she thought she shouldn't or because she felt she was better; rather, they were in many cases a result of her forced travel to other places. Other than her music preferences (Prince, hip-hop, 1980s rap, country, rock, etc.), she had little exposure to cultural diversity between the ages of nine to about eighteen.

She went to college for her first year at a small private school and was once again surrounded by people who looked just like her. She didn't pick the school for that reason; she picked it because it was close to home and she could go home and see her boyfriend easily on weekends. She left that school after one year and went to a small, highly selective school in the Northeast that was highly diverse. One of her roommates was Hispanic, but again, perhaps because she was naive, it didn't occur to her to ask about her background or heritage. Three months later, she changed schools again and was attending a large public state institution in her home state known for teacher education.

She always had aspirations to become an educator, and finally she was smart enough to choose a college for the right reasons. She chose to double major in psychology and chemistry education; she worked almost full time and carried a seventeen-hour course load each semester. Although this was a somewhat diverse environment, her surroundings were filled with students who were White; in fact, she doesn't remember having many true friends that were non-White. Students in her classes, dorm floor, and workplace were predominantly White. She became friends with one African American co-worker, but it never occurred to her that his life might be any different than hers because of his race; she figured their lives were a little different because she was in college and working with no intent to make a career of that job while he was settled into his career and had no intention of going to college, as far as she knew. It is only now that she came to realize the naivetés of such a perspective.

She has her husband to thank for her multicultural evolution and subsequent career success. At age twenty-four she married a reckless, immature, nineteen-year old boy who made her heart pound. He had enlisted in the U.S. Army and was to be stationed at a base in the Southeast. She saw him as a ticket out of the Midwest to a place near the ocean that would be fun and so very different from her present life. She did no research about the town to which they were moving other than to change her student teaching venue to the district in which the base was located and to enroll in the university that would supervise her student teaching.

When they arrived, she was shocked. For the first time in her life she was living in a place with more diversity than she ever remembers seeing except on trips at least an hour outside of town. She was introduced to her cooperating teacher just before school started, and it didn't occur to her to ask questions about the school other than what courses she would be required to teach. Although her cooperating teacher, her supervising university professor, and the school principal were all White, there were African American teachers, administrators, secretaries, and custodians. It did not take long to realize that things were much different at this school than she had expected.

According to Howard's (2006) interpretation of Helms and Piper's six stages of development of White racial identity, she was entering into Phase I: Abandonment of Racist Identity. She was in the midst of the contact stage and most definitely encountering non-Whites in large numbers for the first time. She had no idea that she had been so completely unaware of her Whiteness until that day. While she cannot tell you exactly how she felt that day, she is sure it was a mixture of surprise and concern. She sincerely hoped it was nothing more negative than that.

She had no idea that other people saw her as White or that being White somehow made her life fundamentally different from theirs. She had no idea at the time that her ignorance of White privilege was so profound. Nonetheless, the science department took her under their collective wing, White and Black alike, and did everything they could to help her succeed. She got along well with nearly all of them and felt as if she had several "moms" away from home. She must have heard the southern expression "Bless her heart!" hundreds of times in reference to her ignorance of diversity.

She remembers feeling scared to death on the first day of school when the kids arrived, and looking back, she is ashamed to admit why she was scared. She makes no excuses for her ignorance, but never in her life had she seen more than twenty-five or thirty non-White people in one place in close proximity at the same time. It was overwhelming to be surrounded in the halls by hundreds of African American, Hispanic, Asian, and kids of mixed races that she had never seen before in her twenty-four years of life. She was scared of the unknown, and she thinks that was the first time that she really realized that she *was* different and that the students would know by looking at her that she was different. She has come to learn that this is pretty typical White egocentrism.

The other really scary aspect of the situation for her was the level of security at the school. Growing up, she never saw a police officer in a school, so she was alarmed to find a police officer whose sole job was to be at the school every day for the entire school day. In her high school years she witnessed just one fight. There was no need for metal detectors at sporting events; in fact, she never attended any event where metal detectors were used. She never saw drugs, drug-sniffing dogs, or witnessed anyone get arrested at school. She saw and experienced all of these things during her student teaching. Unfortunately, she initially attributed the need for increased security to the fact that there were so many Black students.

During this time of student teaching, she got to know kids and they got to know her. For the most part, it was a really good experience. While she recognizes that she wasn't the greatest teacher during that time, her fears were short-lived as she quickly realized the students were just regular kids; in fact, they were similar to her in many ways. Like all kids, they didn't behave all the time; although she wishes she could say she never attributed their bad behavior to anything other than poor choices, she has serious doubt that she didn't attribute it to their race and socioeconomic (SES) statuses because all she knew in comparison was her high school experience. In her high school, students behaved and were respectful to the teachers almost all of the time— at least during class, anyway. Rarely did any of them question a teacher, but they were also all White. Reflecting on her experiences in a predominantly White environment, she believed that her new students were ill behaved because they weren't White.

She finished her student teaching and was excited to take a job teaching chemistry at that same school, where she worked for five more years. She developed distinctly different relationships with teachers and students. Her closest colleagues were White teachers; she guesses that just seemed normal to her and it seemed as though they had more in common. But as an athletic coach for all five years in that school, she developed many close relation-ships with students of varying races and ethnicities. Like many in the contact stage, she thought that being "color blind" was the least racist thing she could do and the best way to show that she saw all kids as being equal (Howard, 2006). Again in her naivety, she really did believe that kids were kids and the fairest approach was to treat them all the same.

She remembers going home to her small Midwest town and telling family and friends that she worked in a school that had more kids in one district than her entire hometown. She remembers having to defend working in a place that was about 60 percent minority and explaining how that was really okay and that the kids for the most part were "just like us." She remembers trying to distinguish for her family the difference between the Black kids and the "niggers," which some of her friends called African Americans. She remem-bers feeling surprised by their stereotypical questions, but she also remem-bers thinking many of the same things in her early days at that school, disclosing this to only her closest friends. Although she doesn't use the "n" word, she is sure she made some of the same assumptions about the "good" kids being more "White" than their ill-behaved counterparts.

It was during her tenure at this school that she also entered into the disintegration stage (Howard, 2006), in which one begins to come to grips with Whiteness and question what they may have been raised to believe.

Sadly, she thinks she was stuck in this stage for many years, for although she began to question what she believed and thought, she had absolutely no idea how to answer her own questions, and she had no one to really ask, so she doesn't think it even occurred to her to do so for quite some time. Despite later going to a historically black college and university (HBCU) to get her master's in administration, she remained in the infancy of the disintegration stage.

After completing her graduate degree, she was able to get a job as an assistant principal right away. She went to work in another big high school, a brand new school in the same district that was probably 60 percent White and only about 25 percent lower SES status. She honestly thinks she digressed in her journey while at this school. She developed a few close friendships with others who were not White, and they never questioned her race.

She had fewer strong relationships with the kids because she didn't coach or teach them directly; in fact, most of their interactions were a result of disciplinary measures that got them sent to her office. While she continued to have lots of "contact," *she* did not get any questions answered that developed in the disintegration stage, and she quite frankly put them aside. No one seemed to notice or care that she was perfectly comfortable with being White, and during those years she developed quite a reputation for treating kids well and fairly even when she had to discipline them.

In the spring of 2005, she was chosen to be the principal of a new innovative high school that would be located on the same HBCU campus where she completed her graduate work. The school was designed to attract first-generation college students, which meant their parents did not have a four-year degree. During the interview process, she remembers thinking administrators would want an African American principal because of the school's location, but she interviewed anyway, thinking she had nothing to lose because she loved her current job.

Never once did she really give thought to the fact that attracting first-generation students would most likely mean a student body that was overwhelmingly minority and low-SES status. In a way it was actually better that she never considered it, because she saw this as a job that would open doors and help kids attain more in life than they might otherwise expect. It mattered not what the kids looked like; she just wanted to be part of helping them.

It was during the first few months of this new job that the resurgence into the disintegration stage really took hold for her. She immediately began, with the help of the training and staff development that was part of this new innovative school, to question the activities and beliefs that she thought were helpful to kids. She began to see previous actions as limiting, and although at the time she hadn't thought them evidence of blatant racism, she began to realize it probably was more like institutionalized racism, and she bought into it willingly. During her first year as school principal, she had the good fortune to work closely with a talented African American counselor. Finally, she had someone whom she could trust with her "stupid" questions about non-White cultures and races that were so foreign to her despite having worked in a very diverse district for almost a decade.

It was then that she really learned about African American cultural experiences and began to gain an understanding of how children, parents, and grandparents interacted. It was also the place where she was really indoctrinated into the world of lower-SES status kids and just how detrimental that can really be to a child's education. She got a firsthand look at the difficulty a low-SES child may have in completing tasks that are often designed for kids without those struggles. She also began to see that oftentimes teachers who don't understand the struggles of kids from lower socioeconomic backgrounds may appear to be oppressive.

The third stage for Helms and Piper (Howard, 2006) is the *reintegration* stage, during which one might regress to previously held prejudice and racist beliefs. It is here that White supremacy, whether blatant or not, may be embraced. She did not experience this stage, but rather, as Howard (2006) indicates is possible, moved right into the *pseudo-independent* stage. In this stage a White person's attempts to abandon racism manifests in helpfulness toward those from other races. In this stage, however, there is no focus on changing the dominance patterns that may be systemic in a particular school or policy.

She lived in this stage for two solid years, dedicating herself to creating a school team that helped both non-White and White children. Again, through the staff development tied to her innovative school, the team created what was to become a model in the state based on the test scores, low dropout rate, students' success in college coursework, and the development of teaching practices that reach out and embrace students. The team created a place that was meeting the needs of non-White and White students alike.

During the third year of her principalship, she felt comfortable enough to go back to school to get her doctoral degree in Educational Leadership. She attended the same HBCU where she earned her master's degree and where her current school was housed. During her coursework she found she had really begun to evolve racially, so to speak. During a class called Cultural Diversity in American Schools, she was introduced to the ideas of Whiteness and White privilege, and this marked her entry into the *immersion/emersion* stage (Howard, 2006), in which one moves from just trying to help other races to trying to change oneself and others in positive ways. This stage is about being proud of being White (in her case) but not being racist in action, whether blatant or not.

While reading *Becoming and Unbecoming White* (O'Donnell, 1999), she was particularly struck by the similarities to her own progression. In the text, O'Donnell describes himself as a "tourist," living and working in a diverse community and school but not feeling that he really "lived" there. For the first decade or so of her life in the Southeast, she, too, felt she was just a "tourist" in terms of her own racial identity and development as a culturally diverse person.

She also related to O'Donnell's need to see racism existing places other than the obvious (KKK, White supremacy groups, Nazi Germany, etc.). Until she was into her doctoral coursework, she had no idea that racism could be subliminal and so well embedded into everyday activities that it goes unnoticed or ignored by many who aren't affected by its outcomes. Whether in her finance class (equity versus adequacy) or organizational theory, her eyes were truly opened to things she just didn't know existed.

Her doctoral coursework introduced her to institutionalized racism in the educational system and the idea that although she genuinely had no idea what she was doing was racist. She had contributed to racism against children for many years as a teacher and administrator. Her immersion in critical educational theory and multicultural education has led her to read books and articles by Howard (2006), Nieto and Bode (2012), and O'Donnell (1999), which really resulted in personal epiphanies and growth. She does not for a second think her journey is complete; rather, it has only just begun.

CONCLUSION

One of the scariest thoughts about this whole process has been the "what if?" What if she had stayed in the Midwest town in which she grew up? Would she have ever learned these things, or would this process have just occurred much later in life? Even scarier is the fact that she made it through almost twelve years in a very diverse environment surrounded by a multitude of races and yet she still managed to be oblivious to what really happens and why it happens.

She never gave thought to the fact that the first people educated were rich, White, male property owners. We are still using a lot of their ideas to teach non-White students, which is problematic because it means that we are trying to educate everyone according to a Eurocentered perspective. If school leaders are really going to transform schools so that they are just and equitable, they will need to reexamine the history of the United States.

It is in critiquing the lies we have been told that White school leaders can develop an understanding of the diverse student groups that have historically been disempowered through what has been called education. Our job as educators in the new century will be to learn more about the experiences of marginalized students that enter our schools. It is the only way that we can truly lead students; besides, *we can't lead students we don't know!*

REFLECTIVE STEPS FOR EDUCATIONAL LEADERS

1. Attend antiracist workshops that can potentially assist with eradicating racism and White supremacy.
2. Identify the numerous ways White privilege may be present in your school.
3. Observe the backgrounds of teachers at your school to see if they have experiences with diverse populations of students.
4. Observe the pictures on bulletin boards in teacher's classrooms. The bulletin boards might offer some idea about a teachers' philosophy. Think about the pictures you might display in your office as the educational leader.
5. Build a library of books that examines critical White studies.
6. Create professional learning communities that specifically speak to eradicating racism.

DISCUSSION QUESTIONS

1. What are your initial thoughts about this White educational leader's experiences as a school leader?
2. How might the study of race and racism be beneficial to educational leaders from diverse backgrounds?
3. Do you think it is possible for non-White educational leaders to perpetuate many of the injustices described in this chapter?
4. Do you think it is important for educational leaders to have discussions about racism in their preparation programs?

REFERENCES

Howard, G. (2006). *We can't teach what we don't know: White teachers, multiracial schools* (2nd ed.). New York: Teachers College Press.

Nieto, S., & P. Bode. (2012). *Affirming diversity: The sociopolitical context of multicultural education* (6th ed.). Boston: Pearson.

O'Donnell, J. (1999). The recollections of a recovering racist. In C. Clark & J. O'Donnell (Eds.), *Becoming and unbecoming White: Owning and disowning a racial identity* (pp. 137–49). Westport, CT: Bergin & Garvey.

Young, M., & J. Laible. (2000). White racism, anti-racism, and school leadership preparation. *Journal of School Leadership* 10, no. 5: 374–415.

Chapter Four

Multicultural Education, Curriculum, and Critical White Studies for Educators

Abul Pitre and Esrom Pitre

INTRODUCTION

While demographically America is undergoing major changes that will ultimately result in non-Whites being the majority population in the United
States, public school curricula has remained insufficient when it comes to
addressing multicultural education. Curriculum scholars have noted that at
the heart of education is the curriculum (Kliebard, 1995; Pinar, 2012; Tanner
& Tanner, 1990). English (2000) indicates that to be effective in schools, a
curriculum must have at least three essential characteristics: it must provide
for consistency (coordination), continuity (articulation), and flexibility as
teachers interact with students.

What is apparent from examining the work of curriculum scholars is that
teachers play a significant role in determining how students will experience
the curriculum. What happens when teachers have totally different life experiences from the students they teach? Do teachers who have dysconscious
racism (King, 1991) alienate non-White children from school? With these
pressing questions, school leaders who are committed to creating a culture of
learning need to acquire the knowledge and skills to integrate multicultural
education into the school curriculum.

Multicultural education offers a possibility for the overwhelmingly White
teaching force to reexamine their assumptions and beliefs while at the same
time gaining a more accurate historical account of American history. Sleeter
(2004), speaking to the historical necessity of multicultural education, posits
"white people need to learn about racism, as well as about the historic experi-

ences and creative works of minority groups and about the wide range of implications for schooling. This means beginning their reeducation by forcing them to examine White privilege" (p. 176). Thus, multicultural education could serve as a way for educators to revisit the lies they have been told. A powerful critique of the *official story*—the story sanctioned by those in the dominant group—has failed to mention lynching, prison rape, and genocidal U.S. policies aimed at oppressed groups, which could move educators to construct new ways of thinking about schooling and education (Pinar, 2012).

The No Child Left Behind Act of 2001 has created a phenomenon whereby school leaders have become more concerned with test scores, diminishing the role of multicultural education in the schools. In efforts to meet *adequate yearly progress*, schools have become more punitive for those students who have been historically marginalized. As a result, some students are resisting oppressive schooling that seeks to silence them, thus creating a hostile learning environment.

Sergiovanni (1999) correctly identifies that a major problem with schools is that they have become too bureaucratic and have thus lost their lifeworld and become colonized. Unfortunately, at the center of the colonization of schools are the students who have been colonized by the monocultural curriculum that supports White supremacy.

In this chapter, we offer a vision of multicultural education that allows school leaders to address issues such as the majority White female teaching force, the role of colleges of education in preparing White teachers, and the shortage of non-White teachers in school districts. Included in our critique is a discussion of White studies as an important aspect of helping educators deconstruct notions of White supremacy.

The primary reason that we focus on White teachers is because they make up the majority of the teachers in public schools. We realize that non-White teachers may have developed Anglo-Saxon views of the world that are described by Banks (2014) when he says, "Some individuals of color in the United States such as many African Americans, Native Americans, and Puerto Rican Americans in their effort to assimilate and to participate fully in mainstream institutions, become very Anglo-Saxon in their ways of viewing the world and in their values and behavior" (p. 3). Thus, we hope not to offend but to stimulate a critical perspective. Nieto (2004) succinctly describes the critical perspective of this chapter: "Multicultural education is rightly perceived as a threat because it encourages 'dangerous discourses' and challenges existing arrangements in and out of school" (p. 195).

WHITE TEACHERS AND WHITE STUDIES

In discussing the role of curriculum, one of the major questions scholars encounter is how students will experience the curriculum. We argue that how students experience the curriculum is not solely determined by prepackaged activities listed in curriculum guides but is also impacted by the teacher. With a teaching force that is nearly 90 percent White, how will non-White students experience the curriculum, particularly if their cultural experiences are completely different from their teachers? With this in mind, school leaders need to address the crisis of cultural incongruence.

If schools are going to truly educate all students, it becomes important to examine the impact that White teachers have on the schooling experiences of non-White students. Pitre (2011) disclosed how White teachers placed African American males in special education. The students indicated that their teachers didn't understand their cultural backgrounds and as a result saw them as pathological. Two students described their experiences thus:

> Other special education teachers treated me like I was in jail. They walked me to lunch, to the restroom, to other teachers' classes. I felt like I was in prison on a school campus. No teacher ever explained why they did this; they treated me like criminals are treated. They didn't care. Most of them told me I would be dead by the time I was eighteen or nineteen.

> This teacher yelled at me my first day in her class. She told me sit my ass down. I was mad. I didn't want to stay in her class. She didn't care. All she wanted was for us to sit quietly while she worked on the computer or talked on her cellular phone. My teachers in special education made me feel like, "He ain't going to learn, he is stupid." That made me feel like . . . man, like I'm dumb, like I couldn't keep up. All my teachers said they would help me get out of special education but none of them did.

The study highlighted how teacher racism played a significant role in African American males' experience of school and accounted for their overrepresentation in behavior disorder classes.

With regard to how students experience the curriculum, consider a class session devoted to Dr. Martin Luther King Jr. During this session the students read through Dr. King's famous "I Have a Dream" speech and watch a video clip of the speech, after which the teacher begins with the following prompt: *Dr. King believed all people should be treated equally regardless of their race. We have progressed a lot since the time of Dr. King. Today all people have equal opportunities for success. Please make a list of how we have advanced as an American society.*

The class is all Black, and the students come from the local housing projects. One of the students raises his hand and says, *We haven't made any*

*progress. Things are just disguised better to give the appearance that every-
thing is all right. Look at most of us who live in the projects; tell me, how
have we progressed ?* The White teacher becomes very upset and responds,
*You have an African American president. The reason you are in the projects
is because of the choices that you make. Anybody can make it in America if
they just work hard and get a good education. President Obama is a good
example.* In this scenario the White teacher, believing the myth of American
equality, has failed to provide a critique of the current social order that
speaks to the needs of the Black students in her class. Instead of using Dr.
King as an emancipatory example of fighting against injustice, the teacher
relies on her Eurocentered perspective, which disempowers her students.

Consider another example: The students are excited about the election of
Barack Obama as the first African American president. They begin to hold a
conversation about it before class: *I am so excited that we have elected our
first African American president!* The teacher, overhearing the conversation,
starts the class by saying: *What do you think about our newly elected president?* The students who were talking shout out: *He is the first African
American president. We are happy.* The teacher responds: *He is not African
American; he is White. His mother was White, and he was raised by his
White grandparents. You would do better saying he is biracial.* The teacher
has just deflated any conversation that could lead to a discussion about issues
such as change and social justice that seemed to permeate the presidential
campaign.

Non-White students who experience the aforementioned scenarios might
begin to resist schools. The African American male students who are leaders
will not sit idly by and let teachers make such accusations. Some may refuse
to participate in class, making the teacher angry over her inability to make
the students assimilate to White supremacist thinking. As a result, the teacher
may begin to target the leaders of the class. In conversations in the teacher's
lounge, the White teacher might begin to discuss particular students, leading
to racial profiling in the school and a possible end result of placement in
special education or school suspension.

According to Gay (2004), historically marginalized students do not find
school exciting or inviting. These students often feel unwelcome, without a
sense of belonging because of the Eurocentered curriculum that they view as
irrelevant. This becomes very frustrating for White teachers who assume that
they are doing great work in liberating oppressed students, never realizing
that their views may reflect a White supremacist view similar to that used in
colonizing and enslaving non-White populations. While the curriculum may
be prepackaged, teacher discourse in the classroom plays a significant role in
how students experience the curriculum.

Unfortunately, too many White teachers may be clueless when it comes to
the history of oppressed groups in America. Even more disheartening is that

some teachers may confuse liberation pedagogy with a White missionary zeal to make non-White students view the world from their perspective. The reality is that in too many cases schools for non-White students "force members of these groups to experience 'self alienation' in order to succeed" (Banks, 2014, p. 3).

Woodson (2008) wrote that the worst sort of lynching was taking place in the schools where Black children were being taught that their Blackness was a curse. With a majority White teaching force, one has to wonder about the future of non-White children who are being schooled by White women teachers "who may hold a different sociopolitical, socio-cultural, and socioeconomic perspective" (Hancock, 2006, p. 97). Kunjufu (2006) cogently writes that the future of Black people is "in the hands of White female teachers" (p. 11). This powerful statement presents a problem for school leaders primarily because the experiences of students of color may be greatly different from those of White teachers. The dilemma is exacerbated in the South where the student population is majority non-White. Historically, the South has served as a hotbed of racism for non-White citizens, illuminating the need for educators to engage in critical multicultural education discourse on racism (Gollnick & Chinn, 2012).

Multicultural education offers White educators an opportunity to develop deep insights into institutional racism while also reflecting on their personal beliefs. Howard (2006) cogently describes this self-reflective moment as a period where White teachers can address their "crazy uncle" who has been held in the closet because he is a racist. In some cases the crazy uncle has become a part of the psyche of some White educators; thus, to dislodge him would mean an exorcism.

A society historically rooted in White supremacy creates a phenomenon where some White teachers may not even realize that their racist "uncle" has been internalized in their psyche. The institutional structures that perpetuate racism are so deeply engrained into the society that White educators may be unconscious of its existence. According to Taylor (2009), "Whites cannot understand the world that they themselves have made. Their political, economic, and educational advantages are invisible to them and they may find it difficult to comprehend the non-White experience and perspective that White Domination has produced" (pp. 4–5).

To effectively address the dysconscious racism that White educators may experience, it becomes imperative that multicultural education include White studies, a recent area of study that examines the formation of White identity. One of the major goals of White studies is to help dislodge the White supremacist mind-set that has created inequality, oppression, and death for those who are non-White.

White studies offers White educators an opportunity to become something new and different in terms of how they view the world and their interactions with non-Whites. This involves overthrowing the oppressor consciousness, ultimately helping White educators to take on the qualities of emancipatory educators.

One of the main areas that may offer some help to White educators is *culturally responsive teaching.* To perhaps reach a balance between the cultural incongruence that exists between White educators and non-White students, culturally responsive teaching requires educators to incorporate the cultural experiences of students into their pedagogy (Ladson-Billings, 2008). Culturally responsive teaching offers a way to bridge the academic curriculum to what students already know. In addition, it takes a social justice approach to education that attempts to make students conscious, deliberative, and active about the inequality that exists in the society.

Gollnick and Chinn (2012) propose that educators gain knowledge about the cultural experiences of students. Students' cultural background should be reflective in the examples used to teach academic concepts; for example, rural students do not relate to riding a subway to school or work, nor do inner-city students easily relate to single-family homes with large yards. If students seldom see representations of themselves, their families, or their communities, it becomes difficult to believe that the academic content has any meaning or usefulness for them.

To effectively ensure that multicultural education permeates everything that happens in K–12 schools, colleges of education will have to play a central role. Vavrus (2002), speaking to the challenge facing colleges of education regarding multicultural education discourse on racism, posits, "A teacher education program is an important location for teacher candidates and in-service teachers to become more knowledgeable about theories and practices supporting reductions in racism" (p. 74). Gay (2005) notes the Eurocentric curricula in colleges of education: "Like teacher education, most curriculum designs and instructional materials are Eurocentric" (p. 228).

A perusal of colleges of education reveals that one course on multicultural education may not be enough to help teachers dislodge racist tendencies; thus, it will become important for colleges of education to find ways to ensure that discourse on multicultural education permeates several courses that students take. To address these issues, it may be necessary for colleges of education to change the curriculum for education majors to one that includes required courses in African American studies, Women's studies, Hispanic studies, and others. Rather than offering humanities and social science courses that are largely taught by professors who may have a Eurocentered focus, colleges of education could have students take courses in ethnic studies, which could perhaps alleviate the problem of "race talk" that education professors often describe as a complicated conversation.

Some professors have disclosed how their students usually become combative or silent on issues of race (Boyer & Davis, 2013; Howard, 2006;

Sleeter, 2004). One of the reasons for such may be that they have been socialized to see education as being neutral, and thus in their coursework they do not expect to hear critical conversations about racism or social class issues. Courses in ethnic studies would create a different mind-set for prospective teachers and school leaders as they would have some knowledge that these courses are going to deal with issues around the schooling experiences of non-White students to address racism (Vavrus, 2002).

In addition to revising the course curriculum for education majors, there is a need to recruit more non-White teachers. Hancock (2006) contends, "Desegregation policies were forged in many cities by closing predominately African American schools, busing Black students to segregated White schools, and demoting or firing African American teachers and administrators" (p. 95). The White power structure skillfully implemented policies that weaned out Black educators under the disguise of teacher licensure.

The National Teacher Examination—or, as some have called it, the Negro Teacher Eliminator—seems to have fulfilled a need similar to that which surfaced in the boarding schools that Native American children were forced to attend. The motto in those boarding schools was "kill the Indian, keep the man." Thus, the apple that symbolizes education represents what White education would do for Native American people: allow them to keep their outer appearance but turn them completely White on the inside. Unless there is a concentrated effort to recruit more non-White teachers, non-White students may continue to experience inequitable schooling.

CONCLUSION

Because schools are increasingly diverse, the challenge for White educators will be to engage in a historical journey that will allow them to view the world from the perspective of non-Whites. Deconstructing the Eurocentered schooling, while painful, can help White educators become something new and in turn create an educational reform movement whereby all children can experience equality of education.

Multicultural education can help White educators abandon notions of White supremacy to become allies against racism and can encourage them to become authentically invested in the creation of a more equitable society. School leaders will play a significant role in moving schools beyond a human relations approach to multicultural education to one that addresses both individual and institutional racism.

These are indeed challenging times for school leaders who are straddled with layers of bureaucratic mandates, prepackaged curricula, and teacher-student incongruence. How school leaders address multicultural education will be essential to ensuring that all students experience equality of education. It will require leaders to develop antiracist programmatic approaches, which "means being mindful of how some students are favored over others in school policies and practices such as the curriculum, choice of materials, sorting policies, and teachers' interactions and relationships with students and their families" (Nieto & Bode, 2012, p. 45).

REFLECTIVE STEPS FOR EDUCATIONAL LEADERS

1. Review the curriculum content to see how it aligns with student experiences at your school.
2. Provide professional development to help teachers deconstruct negative perceptions they may have of historically underserved students.
3. Develop a student advisory group to discuss curriculum and instructional issues. This could provide educational leaders with some understanding regarding student's curriculum and instructional experiences at the school. How are students experiencing the curriculum and instruction at your school?
4. Develop a lecture series around critical multicultural education and critical White studies.

DISCUSSION QUESTIONS

1. How might White teachers who hold a different sociopolitical perspective impact the achievement of Black students?
2. The case example of the teacher's response to President Obama's election is problematic. Do you think the problem is race or is it cultural incongruence?
3. How are students experiencing the curriculum and instruction at your school?
4. How can you diminish the cultural incongruence between White female teachers and Black males?
5. What are your thoughts about leading culturally responsive teaching for an entire school?
6. Reflecting on your educator preparation program, do you recall any in-depth discussion about racism?
7. How can an educational leader create a culture that is oppressive or liberatory?

REFERENCES

Banks, J. A. (2014). *An introduction to multicultural education* (5th ed.). Boston, MA: Pearson.

English, F. W. (2000). *Deciding what to teach and test: Developing, aligning, and auditing the curriculum.* Thousand Oaks, CA: Corwin Press, Inc.

Gay, G. (2004). The importance of multicultural education. *Educational Leadership* 61, no. 4 (January): 30–36.

Gay, G. (2005). Educational equality for students of color. In J. Banks & C. Banks (Eds.), *Multicultural education: Issues and perspectives* (5th ed.) (pp. 211–38). Hoboken, NJ: Wiley & Sons.

Gollnick, D. M., & P. C. Chinn. (2012). *Multicultural education in a pluralistic society* (9th ed.). Boston, MA: Pearson Education.

Hancock, S. (2006). White women's work: On the front lines in urban education. In J. Landsman & C. Lewis (Eds.), *White teachers/diverse classrooms: A guide to building inclusive schools, promoting high expectations and eliminating racism* (pp. 93–121). Sterling, VA: Stylus Publishing.

Howard, G. (2006). *We can't teach what we don't know: White teachers, multiracial schools* (2nd ed.). New York: Teachers College, Columbia University.

King, J. (1991). Dysconscious racism: Ideology, identity, and the miseducation of teachers. *Journal of Negro Education* 60, no. 2: 133–46.

Kliebard, H. (1995). *The struggle for the American curriculum, 1893–1958* (2nd ed.). New York: Routledge.

Kunjufu, J. (2006). *An African centered response to Ruby Payne's poverty theory.* Chicago, IL: African American Images.

Ladson-Billings, G. (2008). The power of pedagogy: Does teaching matter? In J. Noel (Ed.), *Classic edition sources: Multicultural education* (2nd ed.) (pp. 111–15). Boston, MA: McGraw-Hill.

McLaren, P. (2015). *Life in schools: An introduction to critical pedagogy in the foundations of education* (6th ed.). Boulder, CO: Paradigm.

Nieto, S. (2004). Critical multicultural education and students' perspectives. In G. Ladson Billings & D. Gillborn (Eds.), *The RoutledgeFalmer reader in multicultural education* (pp. 179–200). London and New York: Routledge Falmer.

Nieto, S., & P. Bode (2012). *Affirming diversity: The sociopolitical context of multicultural education* (6th ed.). Boston, MA: Pearson Education.

Pinar, W. (2012). *What is curriculum theory?* (2nd ed.). Mahwah, NJ: Lawrence Erlbaum Associates.

Pitre, E. (2011). *Locked in: African American males in special education.* New York: Linus Publications.

Sergiovanni, T. (1999). *The lifeworld of leadership: Creating culture, community, and personal meaning in our schools.* San Francisco, CA: Jossey-Bass.

Sleeter, C. (2004). How White teachers construct race. In G. Ladson Billings & D. Gillborn (Eds.), *The RoutledgeFalmer reader in multicultural education* (pp. 163–78). New York: Routledge.

Tanner, D., & L. Tanner. (1990). *History of the school curriculum.* New York: Macmillan.

Taylor, E. (2009). The foundations of critical race theory in education: An introduction. In E. Taylor, D. Gillborn, & G. Ladson-Billings (Eds.), *Foundations of critical race theory in education* (pp. 1–16). New York: Routledge.

Vavrus, M. (2002). *Transforming the multicultural education of teachers: Theory, research, and practice.* New York: Teachers College Press.

Woodson, C. G. (2008). *The mis-education of the Negro.* Drewryville, VA: Kha Books.

Chapter Five

Responding to the Education Challenge

Critical Black Pedagogy for School Leaders

Abul Pitre

INTRODUCTION

In this chapter, I argue that there is a need to envision a new theoretical approach to the study of educational leadership. The chapter, while specifically focusing on the educational dilemmas of African American youth, delineates a way to respond to these educational challenges using a new theoretical approach called *critical Black pedagogy in education*. The foundation for critical Black pedagogy in education is grounded in Afrocentricity, multicultural education, critical pedagogy, and African American spirituality. It is argued that from these theoretical constructs Black leaders—their leadership style, their teachings, and spiritual fortitude—could serve as the basis for helping educational leaders construct new ways of leading in schools.

WILL TO EDUCATE

In 1991, the late Dr. Asa Hilliard wrote a powerful article titled, "Do We Have the Will to Educate All Children?" The article gave a powerful testimony to the power of the will to educate African American students. Hilliard started by examining Dr. Abdulalim Shabazz, a great African American educator who specialized in mathematics and has been credited with producing half of the African Americans who have PhDs in mathematics and mathematics education.

Hilliard describes Shabazz's philosophy in five words: "Give me your worst ones," meaning, "Give me your worst math students and I will make them brilliant mathematicians." Shabazz never had any training in teacher education, yet his ability to produce some of the most brilliant mathematical minds is a testament to the power of the will. Hilliard argues that the "googly book scripts" and quick fixes that have been applied to teaching do not really scratch the surface of what is needed to educate. What is needed, according to Hilliard, is "the will to educate."

Amazingly, Hilliard's 1991 writing takes on great significance in the twenty-first century. The plethora of problems impacting African American students is momentous. Scholars have pointed out the disparities in test scores, the huge dropout rates, the overrepresentation of African American males in special education, and a litany of other problems associated with educating African American youth.

Asante (2005) alludes to the horrible condition of schools attended by African American students, writing that he "has never seen a school run by Whites that prepares African American children to enter the world as sane human beings" (p. 65). His indictment of the public school system's failure to educate African American students, contrary to popular belief, is quite accurate.

Prior to the No Child Left Behind frenzy, Asante proposed an idea called *Afrocentricity*. His idea was popularized in an article titled, "The Afrocentric Idea in Education," which stressed the need for an African and African American perspective in education. Asante's (1991) theory of Afrocentric education has beginnings in the classic works of Carter G. Woodson, W. E. B. Du Bois, Malcolm X, and other significant Black leaders. He clearly articulates Woodson's position, contending that African Americans have been educated "away from their own culture and traditions and attached to the fringes of European culture . . . thus dislocated from themselves to the detriment of their own heritage" (p. 170).

What is needed is a theoretical approach centered on the perspective of Africans and African Americans; enter Afrocentricity, a frame of reference wherein phenomena are viewed from the perspective of Black people. There has been much confusion around Afrocentricity and multicultural education. Many believe that the two are distinctively separate, having nothing to do with each other; on the contrary, Afrocentricity is not against multicultural education but in reality forms the foundation from which multicultural education can begin its thrust. Banks (2014) argues that because Afrocentricity does not posit that an African-centered perspective is the only way to view the world, it lends itself to the tenets found in multicultural education.

The multicultural education movement was brought to birth by the Black movement in America, which included Black nationalists and civil rights activists. These two powerful ideological forces consumed the American consciousness, disrupting the entire social order of America. Similar to Black activists who were concerned about Black education, the multicultural education movement argues for the need to restructure educational systems so that they are just and equitable for all children.

Nieto and Bode (2012) provide additional analysis in describing multicultural education within a sociopolitical context. They give the multicultural canon an additional thrust, arguing that multicultural education is antiracist, basic education, important for all students, pervasive, and involves social justice, a process, and critical pedagogy. Contrary to popular belief, multicultural education is not only about learning the culture of various groups that make up the American populace, it also argues for understanding the deeper structural flaws that perpetuate inequality in the schools. At the heart of examining these flaws is critical pedagogy.

Going back to the roots of critical pedagogy, Nieto and Bode (2012) argue that although those coming out of the Frankfurt school of thought may have formally named it, it also has American origins in the work of Carter G. Woodson and W. E. B. Du Bois. I extend this analysis to include Elijah Muhammad, Malcolm X, Marcus Garvey, and other great leaders. Critical pedagogy starts with the idea of examining the relationship between power and knowledge. In this way, one is discerning the origins of the power base by asking who is saying that this knowledge is the most useful.

Apple (2004) posits that official knowledge is the knowledge that the most powerful in the society declare is most important. Watkins (2001) contends that the powerful elite sponsored knowledge with the intent of making Blacks obedient and docile. This sponsored knowledge results in *hegemony*—a position in which the oppressed go along and in some cases contribute to their own oppression. Critical pedagogy offers a compelling opportunity to disrupt the power relations that exist to potentially liberate the oppressed, the marginalized, and even the oppressor.

These powerful theoretical constructs—Afrocentricity, multicultural education, critical pedagogy, and African American spirituality—have tremendous potential to transform schools in a way that a renewed vision for schools could emerge. However, none of these constructs as separate entities has been able to offer a complete vision for a new educational paradigm. It is here that I make the argument that these four ideological constructs could be merged together to form critical Black pedagogy in education.

It is from critical Black pedagogy in education that school leaders may come to envision new schools and a new education, one that has never been experienced before. Thus, critical Black pedagogy in education is composed of the Afrocentric idea, multicultural education, critical pedagogy, and African American spirituality. These four cornerstones represent the possibility of addressing problems related to Black education. Major theorists define these cornerstones:

1. *Afrocentricity* is a frame of reference wherein phenomena are viewed from the perspective of the African person. The Afrocentric approach seeks in every situation the appropriate centrality of the African person (Asante, 1991, p. 171).
2. *Multicultural education* is a process of comprehensive school reform and basic education for students. It challenges and rejects racism and other forms of discrimination in schools and society and accepts and affirms pluralism (ethnic, racial, linguistic, religious, economic, and gender, among others) that students, their communities, and teachers reflect (Nieto & Bode, 2012, p. 44).
3. *Critical pedagogy* asks how and why knowledge gets constructed the way it does and how and why some constructions of reality are legitimated and celebrated by the dominant culture while others are not (McLaren, 2015, p. 197).
4. *African American spirituality* posits that the African concept of life and education require the sacred and the secular to be seen as one. The African worldview does not approach the study of God as some kind of force independent of human reason and physical reality. Instead, it sees God as an inescapable component of human life (Akbar, 1998, p. 50).

The merger of these powerful elements forms critical Black pedagogy in education, providing the possible keys to developing an educational system rooted in the universal principles of freedom, justice, and equality. Kincheloe (2001) may have had such in mind when he contended, "When we use marginalized perspectives as a key ingredient in a critical historical and social studies curriculum, by definition, we study ways of improving the lives of oppressed peoples. Both critical theory and Afrocentricism, though from different cultural traditions, agree on that social educational objective and are willing to work tirelessly to achieve it" (p. 637).

CRITICAL BLACK PEDAGOGY

In this section, I revisit critical pedagogy and propose a new way of approaching the problems of education, particularly Black education, through *critical Black pedagogy in education*. Critical pedagogy is an educational philosophy that focuses on the relationship between power and knowledge, especially as it relates to the education of oppressed peoples. The purpose of critical pedagogy is to address educational, cultural, and moral issues, and by doing so, improve the lives of oppressed people (Kincheloe & Steinberg, 1997; Freire, 2000).

Critical pedagogy is an honest approach to teaching and leading; it does not lend itself to sugarcoating or watering down the harsh realities of everyday life for minority people. Scholars and educators see critical pedagogy as a way to empower students by telling them the truth about groups in America who have been underserved and abused for hundreds of years. Critical pedagogy is a mechanism for constructive social change.

BLACK ROOTS OF CRITICAL PEDAGOGY

The term *critical pedagogy* has roots in the early ideas of Black leaders, scholars, and activists such as Carter Godwin Woodson, the father of American Black history (1875–1950). (See the Chicago Public Library Internet reference for a biography of Dr. Woodson, http://www.chipublib.org/002 branches/woodsonwoodsonbib.html). In 1933 Dr. Woodson authored *The Mis-Education of the Negro*, in which he pointed out that "the education of the Negroes, then the most important thing in the uplift of the Negro, is almost entirely in the hands of those who have enslaved them and now segregate them" (p. 22). Similarly, Paulo Freire (2000), considered by some to be the founder of critical pedagogy, called this a process by which the oppressed were made "beings for others." Woodson (2008) further examined this relationship between power and knowledge when he said, "the thought of the inferiority of the Negro is drilled into him in almost every class he enters and almost every textbook he studies" (p. 2).

In his exegesis of Black education, Woodson was laying the foundation for a critical examination of the Eurocentered school curriculum that had served the purpose of mis-educating Blacks. Woodson's work met resistance from those who thought that Black history would be divisive. Seventy-seven years later, attempts to implement Afrocentered and multicultural perspectives in America's public schools are still under attack by opponents who believe that this approach to education is anti-American and will lead the country into greater division (Schlesinger, 1991).

A new conservative agenda threatens the possibility of having an Afrocentered and multicultural foundation as essential elements of the school curriculum. An example of this is the No Child Left Behind Act, which has relegated administrators and teachers to mere "commissars." The new legislation, which is founded on high-stakes testing, does not help students to examine power relations and how those power relations marginalize some and benefit others.

Ultimately, the new conservative agenda perpetuates the cycle of mis-education, making students, teachers, and administrators *things*: "For the oppressors, 'human beings' refers only to themselves; other people are 'things'" (Freire, 2000, p. 57). To fully understand and deconstruct the new conservative agenda, essential questions regarding *whose knowledge* and *for what purpose* must be examined by those concerned with equality of education.

Critical Black pedagogues were concerned with these questions as expressed in ideas espoused by W. E. B. Du Bois, Carter G. Woodson, and Elijah Muhammad. Their concerns regarding power and the education of Black children are as relevant today as in their time. The contemporary education of Black children is still controlled by a White ruling elite. A good example of White power in schools is seen in conflicts involving two Louisiana school districts that illuminated the relationship between power and knowledge.

In the late 1990s and in 2006, two school districts in Louisiana were mired in controversy when African American board members attempted to implement Black history courses. At one high school the Black history program and its African American studies course were threatened with elimination by White school administrators despite the program's proven effectiveness in motivating students, reducing student resistance to education, and raising test scores (Pitre et al., 2008; Pitre, 2011).

The majority of the White school board felt that these initiatives had created a consciousness within students that threatened the school's Eurocentric orientation and the institutionalized denigration of Black history and Black contributions to American history. In Lafayette, Louisiana, the school board decided not to incorporate Black history in the schools. The vote was 7–2 against Black history being taught, with the two Black board members voting for Black history implementation (Domingue, 2006). This is evidence of Woodson's prophetic argument that Negroes have no control over their education.

Elijah Muhammad articulated the ideas of critical pedagogy in a very profound way, arguing that those in the dominant positions would never teach Black people the knowledge of self, because this would end the slave-master relationship. He correctly describes the contemporary problem facing historically marginalized students. Despite the positive impact of the critical Black pedagogical curriculum and its positive impact on Black children, it was threatening to some White Americans. Elijah Muhammad brilliantly points out that anyone who performs this great task of awakening Black people will be persecuted. The Louisiana experience demonstrates the validity of Muhammad's words.

Muhammad further argued that to be rulers over rulers requires a superior knowledge. The great fear of the awakening of Black people, or as Elijah Muhammad calls it, "the resurrection," is threatening to those who rule. Muhammad proposed and brought knowledge that was necessary for the resurrection of Black people. Muhammad pointed out that the knowledge of God and self were two necessary components in the awakening of Blacks.

Those who make the educational decisions realize this most important truth regarding knowledge of self and have purposely maintained a curriculum and ideology that reinforces the superiority of Europeans.

Watkins (2005) asserts, "While resistance is inevitable, the dominant ideas of any society are the ideas of its ruling class" (p. 111). This is why certain forms of knowledge must be kept away from the masses. If the masses were given the right kind of knowledge, they would be free from the control of the ruling class. Black history happens to be one of those bodies of knowledge that has remained hidden from everyone, especially Blacks.

Marcus Garvey, like Woodson and Muhammad, asked questions regarding Black education: Where is the Black man's flag? Where is his nation? Where is his army? These questions stimulated Garvey's desire to set up a government for Blacks. Garvey understood that in setting up government, education would be a central component; he therefore urged Blacks to "know" themselves. Garvey's ideas were similar to those of Elijah Muhammad, who stated that Blacks needed an educational system that they could call their own. The problem of power and control highlights the importance of having an independent Black educational system.

CONCLUSION

Critical Black pedagogy in education provides school leaders with a new way of approaching the problem of education by viewing the work of African American leaders. The litany of problems facing African American youth and other marginalized students could be addressed by examining leadership perspectives of great African American leaders. Those concerned with social justice leadership, moral and spiritual leadership, ethics, and critical pedagogy in schools would be well served to examine the leadership styles of Dr. Martin Luther King Jr., Ella Baker, Nannie Helen Burroughs, Malcolm X, Huey Newton, Jesse Jackson, Marcus Garvey, Elijah Muhammad, Louis Farrakhan, Barbara Sizemore, and other Black leaders.

A Eurocentered perspective dominates preparation programs for school leaders and ill prepares them to address the education of disenfranchised youth. It is from a careful study of leadership from multicultural perspectives that school leaders can envision ways of transforming schools so that all children may be led out of darkness into the beautiful light of consciousness that helps them find their purpose in life. Hilliard's discussion of the power of the will brings to mind a long legacy of Black leadership that had to overcome immense struggles.

Historically, it was the will that allowed Black people to survive the cruelties of life intended to dehumanize them. School leaders working from a critical Black pedagogical perspective fueled by willpower could become social justice activists who take action to dismantle the racist, sexist, classist, and dehumanizing school structure that domesticates students for the interest of the ruling elite. To effectively change schools, leaders will need the quintessential characteristic that inspired Black leaders: love. It was a deep love for freedom, justice, and equality that empowered these leaders to lay down their lives for the greater good.

REFLECTIVE STEPS FOR EDUCATIONAL LEADERS

1. Explore the following leadership theories: transactional leadership, transformational leadership, transformative leadership, and servant leadership.
2. Develop a reading list on critical pedagogy.
3. Start a video night where teachers, students, and the community watch videos that empower and raise the consciousness of the school community.

DISCUSSION QUESTIONS

1. What are your thoughts about Afrocentricity? Can White educators be Afrocentric?
2. How would you describe your leadership center (Afrocentric, Eurocentric, neutral)?
3. What are some structural flaws that you have observed in the educational system that create disparities?
4. What are your thoughts about critical pedagogy? What does critical pedagogy mean to educational leaders?
5. What do you think the author means when he says, "It is from a careful study of leadership from multicultural perspectives that school leaders can envision ways of transforming schools so that all children may be led out of darkness into the beautiful light of consciousness that helps them find their purpose in life"?
6. What does love mean to you as an educational leader?

REFERENCES

Akbar, N. (1998). *Know thy self.* Tallahassee, FL: Mind Productions.
Apple, M. (2004). *Ideology and curriculum* (3rd ed.). New York: Routledge.
Asante, M. K. (1991). The Afrocentric idea in education. *Journal of Negro Education* 60, no. 2: 170–80.
Asante, M. K. (2005). *Race, rhetoric, and identity: The architecton of soul.* New York: Prometheus Books.

Banks, J. A. (2014). *An introduction to multicultural education* (6th ed.). Boston: Allyn & Bacon.

Domingue, S. (2006). Black history scratched. *The Daily Advertiser*, June 22, 1, 9.

Freire, P. (2000). *Pedagogy of the oppressed*. New York: Continuum.

Hilliard, A. (1991). Do we have the will to educate all children? *Educational Leadership* 49, no. 1: 31–36.

Kincheloe, J. (2001). *Getting beyond the facts: Teaching social studies/social sciences in the twenty-first century*. New York: Peter Lang Publishing.

Kincheloe, J., & S. Steinberg. (1997). *Changing multiculturalism*. Buckingham, PA: Open University Press.

McLaren, P. (2015). *Life in schools: An introduction to critical pedagogy in the foundations of education* (6th ed.). Boston, MA: Pearson Education.

Nieto, S., & P. Bode. (2012). *Affirming diversity: The sociopolitical context of multicultural education* (6th ed.). Boston, MA: Pearson.

Pitre, A. (2011). *Freedom fighters: Struggles instituting the study of Black history in K–12 education*. San Francisco, CA: Cognella Academic Publishers.

Pitre, A., E. Pitre, & R. Ray. (2008). *The struggle for Black history: Foundations for a critical Black pedagogy in education*. Lanham, MD: University Press of America.

Schlesinger, A. (1991). The disuniting of America. *American Educator* 15, no. 3: 14, 21–23.

Watkins, W. (2001). *The White architects of Black education: Ideology and power in America, 1865–1954*. New York: Teachers College Press.

Watkins, W. (Ed.). (2005). *Black protest thought and education*. New York: Peter Lang.

Woodson, C. G. (2008). *The mis-education of the Negro*. Drewryville, VA: Kha Books.

Chapter Six

Rich Man, Poor Man

Socioeconomic Status and District Wealth as a
Determinant of Student Achievement in Public Schools

Seth Walter Powers

INTRODUCTION

There can be many reasons for below-average student achievement in a school district. Two significant factors in determining student achievement levels are student socioeconomic status and the wealth of a district, the latter of which has been central to a long-standing debate over the funding of public schools in the United States. Ladson-Billings (2009), one of the leading critical race theorists in education, writes, "Perhaps no area of school underscores inequity and racism better than school funding" (p. 31). She goes on to assert that school funding is based on property taxes, which in turn result in funding disparities. As a result, equity and adequacy issues abound when there is the expectation that local communities will pick up where the state leaves off in terms of funding education.

In most cases, local governments finance education through property taxes and, contrary to high-wealth districts, when an area has high poverty and low property values, funds are not available to provide for an equitable education. Almost all states have seen court cases surrounding these issues, and many courts have mandated that states change their funding policies for public schools. In order to draw conclusions of the effect of district wealth on student achievement, an analysis of demographic, fiscal, and achievement data was performed on two New York state school districts: one, a district in New York City, and the other, a suburban district just outside the city in Westchester County.

The central mission of any school or school district is to educate students. Providing an education is what schools do; they give instruction in core curriculum areas as well as in other supplemental areas to educate young people and prepare them to be successful and productive members of society. In America, we even go so far as to mandate that all people are entitled to a free and appropriate public education (FAPE).

Almost every school or district mission statement includes language of assurance that *all* students will learn because as Americans, we emphasize the importance of educating all children regardless of race, ethnicity, gender, socioeconomic status, or disability. We say that every child is important and that all students are entitled to the same opportunities. We are not truthful. America is in reality a country of "haves" and "have-nots."

The "haves" are those citizens, middle class or above, who generally live in modest to affluent areas that are able to support and provide quality education for their children. The "have-nots" come from lower socioeconomic backgrounds and poverty. Some "have-nots" will have access to the same educational opportunities as the "haves," but others will not be so lucky because the circumstances they were born into, such as living in predominantly poor areas, will dictate that they attend school in subpar, sometimes unimaginable, conditions.

Let me describe two schools: School A and School B. School A looks like an architectural dream; in fact, it might not be recognized as a school if not for the sign in front. It is open and spacious on the inside, flooded with natural light, and is more reminiscent of a shopping mall than a school with its atrium area, winding staircase, and food court. Classrooms are bright and clean and are full of up-to-date textbooks, the latest technology, and any instructional materials teachers might need. There are labs for art, science, technology, and vocational classes and a media center to rival any public library. School A is an educational environment to be proud of and makes students feel good just by being inside its walls.

School B is well over a half-century old, and due to a lack of maintenance and proper upkeep it looks every bit its age. Most classrooms are small, dark, and confined with few windows and little natural light. When it rains outside, it rains inside, and many classrooms have large trashcans strategically placed to catch water from the leaky roof. Pipes are exposed, and ceiling tiles and some sheetrock are missing from past leaks. Students share textbooks that are in some cases decades old, any other instructional materials are sparse, and technology is relatively unheard of. The school library is located in the basement and is really just a 10 x 20 foot converted storage room. There is no school cafeteria, so food is prepared at a separate location and brought in daily. In the winter, coal is shoveled by a custodian into a boiler to provide heat. One building has no inside plumbing, so students have to go outside to access an area that has a restroom.

What do you think about the two schools I have described? Where do you think they are located? Of course, School A is located right here in America. I wish I could say that School B was located in some third-world country, but unfortunately, it, too, is an American institution. In fact, both schools are located in the state of Ohio and were highlighted by Jonathan Kozol (1992) in the book and video, *Savage Inequalities*.

America was founded as a land of equal opportunity for all people, but as evidenced by the two schools described above, adequacy and equity issues in public education continue to be real concerns even in the modern age in which we live. These issues are a stumbling block to student achievement in low-wealth districts and a contributor to the achievement gap between White and minority students. The lack of resources in these districts can be directly correlated to lower achievement levels of students in comparison to more affluent districts.

RELATED LITERATURE

The concept of equity and adequacy in relation to public schools in the United States has long been an issue. Equity requires that all students in a state be treated equally, regardless of wealth or where they live. In terms of school facilities, this means that the quality of a student's school building should not depend on a district's willingness or ability to raise taxes or spend money on school facilities (McColl & Malhoit, 2004). Educational adequacy involves states providing schools with sufficient resources to meet state educational goals and standards. These resources include adequate facilities, and states must fund school facilities programs that assure facilities meet state standards (McColl & Malhoit, 2004).

In recent years the fight to ensure that all students have access to a quality education in terms of resources and facilities has been brought into the public eye more than ever before, partly due to the increase in court cases over the past twenty years challenging the distribution of state funding for facilities (Filardo et al., 2006). Generally, these lawsuits have disputed the disparities found in school facilities attended largely by low-income students. The condition of school facilities in many low-income areas is unsafe and inadequate, and so far, thirty-five state courts have heard cases involving school facility funding (Filardo et al., 2006). In at least eleven of these cases, courts have ordered improvements in funding for school facilities based on the states' constitutional requirement to provide students with equal and decent school facilities (McColl & Malhoit, 2004).

The effect of these court cases can be seen by analyzing the 1994 to 2004 McGraw-Hill construction start data comparing states' per pupil expenditures before and two years after successful school facility finance lawsuit decisions (Filardo et al., 2006). Although most states increased spending for school construction during these years, the states that had successful court cases spent an average of $158 more per student annually than states with unsuccessful cases or no facility-related cases at all. This may seem an insignificant amount before considering that the median annual expenditure per student in 2004 was $680. An increase of $158 represents a 23 percent growth in the median construction expenditures per student (Filardo et al., 2006).

One example of a court case that led to new school construction policies in a state was New Jersey's *Abbott v. Burke* ruling in 1985, one of the first statewide school finance decisions that included remedies for inadequate school facilities and a failing funding system (Filardo et al., 2006). The original ruling and subsequent ruling in the 1990s cited the poor conditions and overcrowding in the state's poorest area schools as evidence of the inequities that existed between low-income and high-income areas (Filardo et al., 2006). New Jersey mandated major changes to its education system that included a new funding formula, core curriculum, a statewide preschool initiative, and programs for at-risk students. The state also implemented a large-scale plan to build and better maintain facilities, particularly in the neediest districts, allocating $8.6 billion for new construction and renovations to its neediest school districts in the year 2000 (Filardo et al., 2006).

It is important to understand why certain districts are unable to adequately fund appropriate resources and facilities for their students. Local school districts are primarily funded through property taxes, with nearly half of all property tax revenue being used for public education (Kenyon, 2007). There is debate in our country over the degree to which public schools should be funded with property tax dollars. Some policymakers and analysts believe that there should be a reduced reliance on property taxation and that states should provide more of the funding for public schools, while others claim that the use of local property taxes is a critical ingredient in effective local government (Kenyon, 2007).

For now, in most states property tax continues to be the main source of local funding for schools. This system continues to perpetuate the distinction between the "haves" and "have-nots" alluded to earlier. Obviously, the more populated the area and higher the property values, the more money that is available to support local schools; however, there is not enough property tax revenue available in areas of poverty to adequately and equitably fund schools.

Areas of low wealth, most often found in rural communities and inner cities, face a number of challenges that wealthy districts do not that can lead to lower student achievement. After poor facilities and lack of resources, which have already been discussed, some of these challenges include lower per pupil expenditures and less-qualified and experienced teachers because of the higher salaries offered in wealthy districts through the payment of bonuses and local supplements.

An example of this can be found in a study that compared three select inner-city schools and three suburban schools in a number of different cities across the country. In New York, one of the cities surveyed, per pupil spending in inner city schools was $1,200 less than in suburban schools, while the average inner-city school teacher salary was $42,385 compared with $72,591 for a suburban school teacher (United States General Accounting Office, 2002). The study revealed that generally, inner-city schools scored lower on state reading assessments than did neighboring suburban schools. New York's average reading assessment score was 653. The average score for the state's inner-city schools was around 630, while the average for suburban schools was close to 700 (GAO, 2002).

The average poverty rate in New York's inner-city schools was around 50 percent, but only 5 percent in the suburban schools (GAO, 2002). Clearly, the differences between inner-city and suburban schools are dramatic. The combination of numbers of high-needs students and less money being spent to educate them creates an inequitable and inadequate educational atmosphere in inner-city schools that leads to lower student achievement.

Such issues are not limited to certain areas but can be found in states across the country. A case study involving seven states (California, New Jersey, Texas, Massachusetts, New Hampshire, Ohio, and Michigan), all but one of which (Michigan) are facing state mandates regarding funding, highlights the degree of states' reliance on property taxation and examines other criteria such as per pupil expenditures, special needs, limited English proficiency, socioeconomic status, and student achievement to help form a picture of education in these states (Kenyon, 2007).

Generally, states with higher per pupil expenditures had higher achievement scores on the 2007 National Assessment of Educational Progress test in fourth- and eighth-grade reading and math. California, which ranks forty-second nationally in per pupil spending, ranks near the bottom on the national tests. Michigan, which ranks sixteenth in per pupil spending, is also in the bottom half in student achievement. It is important to note that there may be some correlation between a state's population of at-risk and special-needs students and reported achievement scores (Kenyon, 2007).

Although the amount of money spent on educating students certainly plays a role in student achievement, it must be applied in the right places to help special-needs and disadvantaged students. If additional money is not going to help those students who need the most support, achievement gains will not be realized. This may be the case in Michigan, where per pupil spending and student achievement scores do not seem to add up.

There are many issues involving the wealth of a school district and how it relates to that district's student achievement. As discussed above, funding to schools varies greatly from district to district and usually depends largely on the property tax base for each district. There has been litigation in almost every state over concerns of equity and adequacy in low-wealth school districts. In some cases, this litigation has led to reforms in state funding of schools that have leveled the playing field for the "haves" and "have-nots"; in other states, however, little has changed and students in poverty-stricken areas continue to receive a subpar education.

The link between school district wealth and student achievement has already been discussed; let us now look more closely at the effects of school district wealth on student achievement by examining the demographic, fiscal, and student achievement data of a New York inner-city school district compared with a suburban New York school district.

SCHOOL DISTRICT ANALYSIS—NEW YORK CITY SCHOOLS, DISTRICT #3

The New York City Public School System is comprised of thirty-one districts containing 1,400-plus schools that serve 1.1 million students (New York Public Schools, 2008). This means that New York City Public Schools are educating nearly one-third of the students in New York State—more children than are enrolled in public schools in forty-six other states (Stiefel et al., 2000). The city's per pupil expenditure for the year 2006 to 2007 was $13,496 (Littlefield, 2008). In 2007, the average salary for a teacher in New York City was $57,354. The city's median household income was $53,514, and the estimated median house or condo value was $311,000 (City-Data.com, 2008). In 2001 the average inner-city property value per student was about $260,000 compared to $918,000 in the average New York City suburb (Duncombe & Yinger, 2001).

The city of New York is made up of five boroughs; some are home to the very affluent while others are home to the very poor. New York City Schools District #3 is made up of forty-one schools located in Manhattan. The district is in an affluent part of the city, which includes much of Park Avenue, Central Park, and Broadway. The district is self-described as succeeding in technology, the core curriculum, and preparing students for college and future job markets. District #3 also prides itself in its athletic programs and a multitude of extracurricular activities that are available to its students. The New York State Education Department has given the district high marks (New York Public Schools, 2008). The data provided for District #3 was taken from the district's state report card and reflects demographics and achievement data for the 2007 to 2008 school year, unless otherwise noted. It is important to realize that although District #3 is in an affluent area of the city, many affluent families choose to send their children to private rather than public schools. Thus, the demographic makeup of the district is not what one might expect for an affluent area, but such an area was chosen in hope of it being more comparable to what might be found in the suburbs.

Of District #3's students, 56 percent are on free or reduced lunch and 10 percent are limited English proficient. The racial makeup of the district is 34 percent African American, 38 percent Hispanic, 6 percent Asian or Pacific Islander, and 22 percent White. Of its teachers, 19 percent had fewer than three years of experience, and 36 percent held a master's degree plus thirty hours or a doctoral degree. In 2005 to 2006, the teacher turnover rate for the district was 18 percent.

In analyzing the student achievement data, it is important first to have a standard by which to compare scores. The New York state average of students scoring at or above proficiency on English/Language Arts and math state assessments for 2007 to 2008 was 69 percent in ELA and 81 percent in math. Student achievement in District #3 was close to but slightly below state averages in these areas. An average of 63 percent of students in grades three through eight scored at a level 3 or 4 on the state assessment in English/Language Arts. Level 3 represents meeting learning standards and level 4 represents meeting learning standards with distinction. On the state assessment in grades three through eight in math, an average of 77 percent scored at a level 3 or 4. In fourth- and eighth-grade science, 71 percent and 37 percent (respectively) scored at least a level 3. At the secondary level, 71 percent of students in English and 68 percent in math scored a level 3 or 4.

SCHOOL DISTRICT ANALYSIS—BRONXVILLE UNION FREE SCHOOL DISTRICT

The Bronxville Union Free School District is located in Westchester County, New York, and is a suburb of New York City. The school district is made up of an elementary, middle, and high school and serves approximately 1,500 students in grades K–12. The town of Bronxville is a very affluent area with an estimated median household income in 2007 of $176,000 and estimated median house or condo value of $1,262,397 (City-Data.com, 2008). The wealth of the area is reflected in the funding of education. Per pupil spending in the district was $20,833, and the average teacher salary was reported at $133,211 (stateuniversity.com, 2009).

Like New York City's District #3, data provided for the Bronxville district was taken from its state report card and reflects demographic and achievement data from the 2007 to 2008 school year. The school district's demographic information reflects what one might expect in a high-wealth community: 0 percent of students were on free or reduced lunch and only 1 percent were limited English proficient. The racial breakdown of students in the district was 92 percent White, 5 percent Asian or Pacific Islander, 2 percent Hispanic, and 1 percent African American. Only 3 percent of teachers in the district had three years or fewer experience, and 68 percent hold a master's degree plus thirty hours or a doctoral degree. The teacher turnover rate for the year 2005 to 2006 was 14 percent.

An average of 95 percent of students in grades three through eight scored at a level 3 or 4 on the state assessment in English/Language Arts, which was twenty-six percentile points above the state average. On the state assessment in grades three through eight math, an average of 97 percent scored at a level 3 or 4, or sixteen percentage points higher than the state average. In fourth- and eighth-grade science, 99 percent and 98 percent (respectively) scored at least a level 3. At the secondary level, 98 percent of students in English and 100 percent in math scored a level 3 or 4. Clearly, the Bronxville Union Free School District is a very high-performing school district.

FINDINGS

In terms of student achievement, the Bronxville district outscored New York City District #3 significantly in all state-tested areas. In grades three through eight English/Language Arts and math, the difference was thirty-two and twenty percentile points, respectively. In fourth- and eighth-grade science the difference was twenty-eight and sixty-one percentile points, respectively. In high school English and math the difference was twenty-seven and thirty-two percentile points, respectively.

Obviously, New York District #3 and the Bronxville Union Free School District are very different in a number of ways. When comparing the two districts, three main differences collectively contribute to the significant achievement gap described above: wealth in terms of socioeconomic status, wealth in terms of per pupil spending, and the number of minority students in the districts. Based on the standard of qualifying for free or reduced lunch, over 50 percent of students in District #3 are poor; no students in the Bronxville district would be categorized as poor based on the same standard. Low socioeconomic status of families in a district or school presents challenges in terms of achievement due to a number of factors.

The difference in per pupil spending is another significant factor in the difference in student achievement between these districts. With Bronxville spending over $7,000 more per pupil per year, these students are going to be afforded the best of every learning opportunity. At the very least, students will be educated in appropriate facilities, have the best of new technology, and have numerous other educational resources that would not be commonplace in lower-wealth districts.

In the Bronxville district 10 percent of students are exceptional children requiring an Individual Education Plan (IEP), but student achievement data show that most of these students are passing state assessments. This leads to the conclusion that high district wealth means more resources to help at-risk or special-needs students and consequently, greater success for these exceptional children. Because of the wealth of the community, students also have better teachers. The average teacher salary in Bronxville is $76,000 higher than the average salary of a New York inner-city teacher, and the higher salary can be paid because the wealth of the local government allows for bonuses and supplements that are not an option in lower-wealth areas. As shown by the statistics reported above, Bronxville's teachers on average had more teaching experience, more educational preparation, and a slightly lower turnover rate than was reported for District #3.

Finally, New York's District #3 is 78 percent minority, compared to only 7 percent in Bronxville. The limited English proficiency needs of some minority students present more of a challenge to learning and can affect student achievement. Additionally, there is generally an achievement gap between minority/disadvantaged students and White students, so an increase in the number of minority students can account for lower achievement scores. All of these findings play a role in the difference in student achievement between the two New York school districts.

CONCLUSION

Without question there are many factors other than district wealth that can directly attribute to the student achievement of a school district; however, it cannot be denied that a district's wealth does directly impact the educational opportunities afforded its students and thus also impacts the learning that takes place as a result. Wealthy districts will be able to offer outstanding facilities, current technology, and plentiful educational resources.

These districts will also be able to attract and retain more qualified and experienced teachers because of the higher salaries they are able to offer. Although wealthy districts do not have as many at-risk students because of the socioeconomic status of their population, they are more equipped to provide the additional resources required by the at-risk or special-needs students they do have.

There are certainly examples of low-wealth schools that are doing very well in terms of student achievement. Some that come to mind are the 90-90-90 schools that are at least 90 percent minority, 90 percent free or reduced lunch, and have 90 percent of students meeting proficiency standards on state assessments (Reeves, 2000). However, a school's status as low wealth does not necessarily mean it is a part of a low-wealth district and is receiving inadequate funding.

For example, there are schools in Moore County, North Carolina, with free and reduced lunch rates at around 85 percent, but overall, the county is considered a high-wealth district because of the tax base from the Village of Pinehurst, Southern Pines, and the surrounding resort areas. Even in cases of low-wealth schools and districts that receive inadequate funding yet are beating the odds by making the most of their available resources and doing well in terms of student achievement, I argue that current forms of school funding are still doing these students an immense injustice. Imagine what these students and schools might be able to accomplish if the per pupil spending in their districts were equal to that of the Bronxville Union Free School District.

REFLECTIVE STEPS FOR EDUCATIONAL LEADERS

1. Compare and contrast campus facilities in a high-income area versus a low-income area.
2. Include in professional learning communities Jonathan Kozol's book *Savage Inequalities*.
3. Review recent court cases on disparities in school facilities.
4. Think about ways to involve the community in facility improvement at your school.
5. Develop an advisory board to seek external funding for facility improvement at your school.
6. Organize alumni to assist with fundraising by sponsoring events that welcome alumni back to the campus. Homecoming is an opportune time to get alumni involved with the school.

DISCUSSION QUESTIONS

1. What can you do as an educational leader to eradicate funding disparities?
2. How might the physical facilities of a school impact students, teachers, and staff morale?
3. What can an education leader do to compensate for rundown facilities that contribute to low morale?
4. Do you think leadership styles are different depending on a school's resources? Explain.

REFERENCES

City-Data.com. (2008). Bronxville, New York. Retrieved June 15, 2009, from http://www.city-data.com/city/Bronxville-New-York.html.

Duncombe, W., & J. Yinger. (2001). *Reforming New York's state education aid dinosaur.* Retrieved June 14, 2009, from http://cpr.maxwell.syr.edu/efap/Publications/reforming_ny.pdf.

Education.com. (2009). Bronxville Union Free School District. Retrieved June 16, 2009, from http://www.education.com/schoolfinder/us/new-york/district/bronxville-union-free-school-district/.

Filardo, M., J. M. Vincent, P. Sung, & T. Stein. (2006). *Growth and disparity: a decade of U.S. public school construction.* Washington, DC: BEST (Building Educational Success Together).

Kenyon, D. A. (2007). *The property tax–school funding dilemma.* Cambridge, MA: Lincoln Institute of Land Policy.

Kozol, J. (1992). *Savage inequalities: Children in America's schools.* New York: Broadway Books.

Ladson-Billings, G. (2009). Just what is critical race theory and what's it doing in a nice field like education? In E. Taylor, D. Gillborn, & G. Ladson-Billings (Eds.), *Foundations of critical race theory in education* (pp. 17–36). New York: Routledge.

Littlefield, L. (2008, December). New York state public school finance: NYSED data for school year 2006–2007. *Room Eight New York Politics.* Retrieved June 15, 2009, from http://www.r8ny.com/blog/larry_littlefield/
new_york_state_public_finance_nysed_data_for_sch%20ools

McColl, A., & G. C. Malhoit. (2004). *Rural school facilities: State policies that provide students with an environment to promote learning.* Arlington, VA: The Rural School and Community Trust.

New York Public Schools. (2008). *New York schools.* Retrieved June 10, 2009, from http://www.newyorkschools.com/districts/nyc-district-3.html.

New York State Testing and Accountability Reporting Tool. Bronxville Union Free School District. Retrieved June 15, 2009, from http://www.nystart.gov/publicweb/District.do?year=2008&county=WESTCHESTER&district=660303030000

New York State Testing and Accountability Reporting Tool. New York City District #3 state report card. Retrieved June 14, 2009, from http://www.nystart.gov/publicweb/District.do?year=2008&county=NEW%20YORK&distict=310300010000

Reeves, D. B. (2000). *Accountability in action: A blueprint for learning organizations.* Denver: Advanced Learning Press.

Stateuniversity.com. (2009). Bronxville Elementary School. Retrieved June 16, 2009, from http://www.stateuniversity.com/elmsed/NY/Bronxville-Elementary-School-Bronxville.html

Stiefel, L., A. E. Schwartz, P. Iatarola, & N. Fruchter. (2000). *Academic performance, characteristics, and expenditures in New York City elementary and middle schools.* Education Finance Research Consortium, New York State Education Department.

United States General Accounting Office (GAO). (2002). *School finance: Per pupil spending differences between selected inner city and suburban schools varied by metropolitan area.* Report to the Ranking Minority Member, Committee on Ways and Means, House of Representatives.

Chapter Seven

Exposing the Socially Embedded Undercurrent of Racism in the American Education System

James M. Bass

INTRODUCTION

This chapter examines how racism has become imbedded in the fabric of higher education and society, and it will attempt to point out how it can be recognized and eradicated. According to Chesler, Lewis, and Crowfoot (2005), studies on higher education institutions reveal that racism permeates nearly every aspect of these institutions. The authors suggest that American schools of higher education have been designed without the input of people from diverse and minority backgrounds.

Even more alarming is that colleges and universities have decided against employing minorities en masse, and the curricula have been designed without their voices. While these historical inequalities began very early in higher education history, they have survived unchanged for generations aided by political, social, and governmental support. With each passing generation, the historical legacy of racism has remained in place. Unfortunately, some educational leaders are unknowingly involved in the practice of racism, making it virtually impossible for these leaders to develop policies that address the problem of systemic racism.

What are the steps educational leaders can take to truly dismantle racism in higher education and make colleges and universities places of *higher learning*? One suggestion is for leaders in higher education to examine ideas presented by people of color as related to their vision of education. Pitre (2008) has developed an interesting theoretical approach called *critical Black pedagogy in education*, which is an examination of the educational ideas of Black leaders as they relate to the education of Black people.

In studying the educational ideas of groups who have been historically marginalized, educational leaders could gain much needed knowledge about how to dismantle the systemic racism that permeates too many higher-education institutions. This chapter contends that a major step in eradicating racism in higher education will need to involve concepts in multicultural education, critical race theory, and critical pedagogy. This chapter starts by discussing the educational ideas of one of the most controversial figures in American and world history—Elijah Muhammad. In this chapter, his educational ideas are juxtaposed with multicultural education and critical theories of education. It then focuses on a review of racism in education and extends the discussion of racism to examine institutionalized racism.

ELIJAH MUHAMMAD, MULTICULTURAL EDUCATION, AND CRITICAL THEORIES OF EDUCATION

Educators have hailed multicultural education as a key to solving problems of racism within schools. However, the philosophies and practices behind many programs implemented in American schools have missed their mark primarily because these programs have kept in place the perspectives of those in the dominant group. If multicultural education programs in America are to be effective, they must change behaviors and attitudes through a systematic reevaluation of how knowledge is constructed.

Critical pedagogy offers an insightful approach to progressive multicultural education programs that examines how knowledge is constructed. Peter McLaren (2015), a leading critical educational theorist, writes, "Knowledge is a social construction deeply rooted in a nexus of power relations" (p. 197). While the term *critical pedagogy* has been coined by European scholars, several African Americans scholars articulated the ideas espoused in critical pedagogy.

One of the leading African Americans who discussed the relationship of power and knowledge was Elijah Muhammad. He articulated the origins of White supremacist education and the ways education was constructed to disenfranchise and dehumanize African Americans. In fact, many of the multicultural education concepts that students currently learn resemble Muhammad's educational philosophy.

There are striking parallels between Muhammad's ideas of education and those of major multicultural education theorists in the field who contend that multicultural education is about justice, equality, and freedom. Elijah Muhammad was also an advocate for these concepts with a specific focus on an education that would empower African Americans and other oppressed people. He critiqued education in a way that enabled his students to become critical thinkers. African Americans such as Malcolm X, who were educated by Elijah Muhammad, became individuals who questioned the prevailing world order of White supremacy. Muhammad's educational ideas were rooted in the knowledge of self, which went beyond simply memorizing facts. It was the knowledge of self that put Muhammad's students on a path for pursuing more knowledge (Pitre, 2008).

In analyzing racism, Muhammad went beyond any explanation that has been given to describe its origin and how it could be uprooted. Pitre (2008) argues, "Elijah Muhammad gave his students insight into the nature of racism and the essence of freedom, justice, and equality. Unlike the multicultural educators who primarily examined and discussed issues of racism concerning education, Elijah Muhammad went into the very root of racism" (p. 23).

Muhammad contended that the racist educational institutions of America had mis-educated African Americans since the days of slavery. Throughout the historical sojourn of Black people in America, they were indoctrinated with a White supremacist view of the world that was directly connected to the curricula taught in educational institutions. Elijah Muhammad called for the introduction of a critical Black pedagogy that would get both Blacks and Whites to examine themselves. To effectively eliminate racism, one would have to uncover its origins and the mind-set that brought racism into existence. This would require insightful or superior teachers who could raise the consciousness of their students.

Realizing this, Muhammad was a staunch proponent of honoring teachers and the teaching profession as one of the most honorable callings one could undertake. In explaining the significance of teachers, Pitre (2008) credits Elijah Muhammad with insisting it was the job of the civilized man to teach civilization to the uncivilized and that this would require teachers to have an understanding of self and God. For Muhammad, highly effective teachers would be those who addressed many areas of multicultural education and emphasized a critical pedagogical approach to teaching. He believed teachers should guide young people to learn more about themselves and use this self-knowledge as a context for examining other cultures.

Pitre (2008), speaking to the spiritual exegetes of Elijah Muhammad, contends that he taught that closeness to God could be achieved by realizing that human life was subject to physical and spiritual laws. When one lives according to the spiritual laws that govern creation, one experiences a peace that ushers in a higher spiritual life. This connection between the physical and spiritual, he argues, helps students create their own heaven on earth. Leaders approaching the education of students as a matter of spiritual concern may offer the possibility for rethinking our philosophy of education, thus creating new school cultures.

Elijah Muhammad was an advocate for a kind of education that would empower Blacks and other oppressed people to become critical thinkers, citizens with a voice to question and explore the world. He opposed education that focused on making Blacks subservient to those in positions of power. In doing this, he critiqued racism in a way that was very similar to that of scholars in multicultural education.

REVIEW OF RACISM

The notion that racism exists within the fabric of the social and educational systems of America is nothing new. Since the 1970s, research has exposed racism and demonstrated how racist agendas have been embedded in the curricula and practices of educational institutions. According to Johnson (1975), the American educational system has socialized norms, behaviors, and attitudes through the hidden curriculum. The author suggests that this has perpetuated racism throughout the entire educational system, resulting in the production of fewer minority educators, which in turn limits access to diverse faculty for growing numbers of students. This kind of system has been reinforced for so long that many of its members do not realize they have been conditioned.

Djangi (1993) published research pointing to the existence of racism within graduate school psychology programs. The author insisted that both covert and overt forms of racism are embedded in educational curricula. Djangi pointed to the many minority students who are also first-generation college students and may benefit from support programs focused on making their college experience successful. He called for programs that make cooperative learning opportunities, and thus cross-racial exposure, possible for students and noted that courses in ethnic awareness might also help address racial issues.

The problem of embedded educational racism is not germane to the United States, according to Gillborn (2009). Conventional forms of antiracism have not been able to keep pace with racist and exclusionary educational policies that are masked by tolerance and diversity claims. Gillborn pointed to critical race theory studies in the United States as a perspective for approaching problems with racism in America, suggesting that it can be used as a means for focusing on the outcomes of positive practices and a way to move past the problems of intent that are blamed on racially charged situations.

Raby (2004) contends racism is often downplayed and considered alien to Whites, suggesting that perceptions of racism are always changing in young people and are sometimes even contradictory to their expressions of racism—making them both racist and antiracist. One strategy for instilling antiracist attitudes and perceptions is to study history—not just historical injustices, but how race is conceptualized and constructed. Also, antiracist educators can demonstrate how unequal and systematic relations of power exist within organizations and social structures to show students how these relationships and systems feed individual acts of racism.

According to Rebollo-Gil and Moras (2006), a practice among Whites is to preface racist comments with a denunciation of racism, or to speak in coded language. Because of such habits as well as a softer criticism of racist practices when employed within common social and familial groups, the authors suggest that White racism is often considered foreign, something that others do. In other words, no social responsibility is claimed. The authors go further to suggest that while White students openly profess that violence and hatred-based racism is wrong, few if any will admit to having benefited by the oppression of racism. They claim that in order to teach White Americans antiracism, educators must talk openly about oppression and teach students to understand both its institutional nature and how it is perpetuated.

Heinze (2008), a White educator, argues that it is important for Whites to first understand White culture and privilege before they can begin to appreciate the cultures of other people. The author says this is important because the experience of many people of color in the United States has been defined by the racist oppression of White America. Heinze also notes that many White Americans do not consider themselves to be racist, but when made aware of their unintentional racist actions, they experience guilt and shame.

According to Denevi and Pastan (2006), the resistance of White Americans to actively combat racism is rooted in White privilege, which the authors call a *cultural manifestation*. They suggest that the only way to change White attitudes about racism is to create more opportunities for introspection and to acknowledge White privilege as something real. Getting White students to hold White-on-White group dialogues can help these students develop antiracist identities. Students and faculty of color at institutions can support this, and the authors suggest that they can become allies of this movement.

Lee (2007) points out that racism in American institutions extends to prejudices toward international students. The author's research shows an imbalance in student exchange programs, with more international students studying in the United States than American students studying abroad. The author further shows that those American students who do study internationally do so in Europe or other Westernized countries and suggests that in order for American students to truly understand what it means to be global citizens, they must gain experience in countries that are not like the United States.

INSTITUTIONALIZED RACISM

Hatch and Cunliffe (2006) propose a framework for understanding how embedded racism can be identified within society and its various agents. According to the authors, people are drawn to different perspectives, and they use different forms of knowledge to understand them. They offer three perspectives for assessing and interpreting organizational theory, presenting a new lens for analyzing how attitudes and beliefs are perpetuated within social networks.

The modernist perspective proposes that external realities can exist without most people ever knowing about it. The symbolic-interpretive approach suggests that to know an external reality outside of our own experience, it is necessary to have a subjective awareness of it. The postmodernist perspective suggests that an organization can exist as long as it is spoken of or referred to through language.

These concepts are featured in the 1999 film *The Matrix* (directed by Andy and Lana Wachowski), in which "real" society exists outside of the constructed alternate reality, or the "matrix," that the characters had come to know. In the movie, individuals must know the difference between the matrix and real life in order to be free and independent (symbolic interpretivism). According to the modernist perspective, the only way for the matrix system to survive is to spread, and this becomes a function and process of the organization. Also in the movie, people become so dependent on the system that some cannot think outside of the program and are willing to fight to keep it alive. The rules of living within the matrix become ways of predicting and controlling human behavior, and those who were aware of and controlling the matrix did not want its unknowing participants to awaken to reality because then they would no longer be controlled.

In the film, the matrix is described as a system that "the mind makes real"; in other words, realities can be socially constructed through the beliefs held by its participants. As people within organizations tend to identify themselves by their membership and language and behavior set members apart from those outside the group, it is unsurprising when a character in the movie says, "If you're not one of us, you're one of them." Identity and race are social constructs; characters in *The Matrix* define their identities based on their relationships within the organizational framework, and that's very similar to what we see within the various societies in America, including the educational system.

In their book, *Challenging Racism in Higher Education*, Chesler et al. (2005) report that studies have been conducted to support the existence of racism embedded into the culture and operations of higher education. This notion may appear contrary to the beliefs of many educators because *diversity* has become such a buzzword on college and university campuses across the country. If schools, colleges, and universities are taking such proactive stances to ensure that diversity is integrated and applied across the curriculum, how could they be accused of being discriminatory? How could racism exist in such an environment that is designed to keep racism out?

CONCLUSION

Gillborn (2009) does not criticize the work that has been done to address equity issues concerning racism in education, but he believes educators must go beyond this if they are to begin eliminating the factors that contribute to racism's systematic existence:

> If we only focus on the scale of inequity and school-level approaches to addressing it, we lose sight of the most powerful forces operating at the societal level to sustain and extend these inequalities. Essentially, we risk tinkering with the system to make its outputs slightly less awful, but leaving untouched the fundamental shape, scale, and purpose of the system itself. (p. 18)

As suggested earlier, one solution to dismantling racism will require an educational approach based on critical race theory as a perspective for assessing embedded racism that focuses on the central idea that racism is embedded legally, culturally, and even psychologically, and that its effects can be seen both in obvious actions and within hidden patterns of behavior that disadvantage minority groups.

Rebollo-Gil and Moras (2006) argue the need for multicultural education to actively attack the stereotypes of minorities that are perpetuated by the media. The authors suggest that if not, "these depictions then foster . . . negative beliefs concerning the social nature of People of Color, which then inform the few real-life encounters [Whites] have with them" (p. 385). They add that beneficial dialogue about racism cannot happen within an insulated group, one that does not include representative dialogue from all members of the community. Since racism is a social construct (Hatch & Cunliffe, 2006), then it can be eradicated. It will certainly be beneficial when antiracist ideas are infused within the curricula of educational programs, ultimately creating a new mind-set in the people of America.

REFLECTIVE STEPS FOR EDUCATIONAL LEADERS

1. Develop a leadership vision grounded in the principles of social justice and equity.
2. Create opportunities to show appreciation for faculty and staff.

3. Develop a multicultural center that provides information about diverse groups of people while simultaneously addressing issues of equity and social justice.
4. Watch the following movies: *Higher Learning, The Matrix*, and *White Man's Burden.*

DISCUSSION QUESTIONS

1. What does knowledge construction imply about leadership?
2. What might explain the reason critical black pedagogues in education are absent from the educational discourse?
3. What does raising the consciousness of students mean to you?
4. Briefly discuss your philosophy of education. Where does your philosophy originate?
5. How might Elijah Muhammad's ideas apply to diverse groups of people?
6. Do you think racism is a social construct?

REFERENCES

Chesler, M., A. Lewis, & J. Crowfoot. (2005). *Challenging racism in higher education: Promoting justice.* Lanham, MD: Rowman & Littlefield.

Denevi, E., & N. Pastan. (2006). Helping whites develop anti-racist identities: Overcoming their resistance to fight racism. *Multicultural Education* 14, no. 2: 70–73.

Djangi, A. (1993). *Racism in higher education: Its presence in the classroom and lives of psychology students.* Paper presented at the American Psychological Association, Toronto, Canada, August 23, 1993.

Gillborn, D. (2009). Critical race theory and education: Racism and anti-racism in educational theory and praxis. *Discourse: Studies in the Cultural Politics of Education* 27, no. 1: 11–32.

Hatch, M. J., & A. L. Cunliffe. (2006). *Organization theory* (2nd ed.). New York: Oxford University Press.

Heinze, P. (2008). Let's talk about race, baby: How a white professor teaches white students about white privilege and racism. *Multicultural Education* 16, no. 1: 1–11.

Johnson, H. (1975). *The educational system as a reinforcer of institutionalized racism.* ERIC.

Lee, J. (2007). Neo-racism toward international students: A critical need for change. *About Campus* 11, no. 6: 28–30.

McLaren, P. (2015). *Life in schools: An introduction to critical pedagogy in the foundations of education* (6th ed.). Boulder, CO: Paradigm.

Pitre, A. (2008). *The educational philosophy of Elijah Muhammad: Education for a new world* (2nd ed.). Lanham, MD: University Press of America.

Raby, R. (2004). There's no racism at my school, it's just joking around: Ramifications for antiracist education. *Race, Ethnicity and Education* 7, no. 4: 367–83.

Rebollo-Gil, G., & A. Moras. (2006). Defining an "anti" stance: Key pedagogical questions about engaging anti-racism in college classrooms. *Race, Ethnicity and Education* 9, no. 4: 381–94.

Ryan, J. (2003). Educational administrators' perceptions of racism in diverse school contexts. *Race, Ethnicity and Education* 6, no. 2: 145–64.

Chapter Eight

Multicultural Education

An Ethical, Moral, and Social Justice Imperative

Abul Pitre

INTRODUCTION

The chapters in this book provide a foundation for a critical study of educational leadership as it relates to critical multicultural education. Multicultural education should inspire school leaders to become more than *technocrats*; it should compel them to have a vision of school that touches the soul of the communities they serve. Multicultural education is an ethical, moral, and social justice imperative for school leaders.

ETHICAL AND MORAL LEADERSHIP

School leaders are bombarded with bureaucratic mandates that are driven by political mechanisms that ultimately make too many schools sites of domestication. Paulo Freire addressed the politics of education, pointing out that "it does not matter where or when it has taken place, whether it is more or less complex; education has always been a political act" (Darder, 2002, pp. 126–27).

Education in the United States, particularly as it relates to students of so-called color, has domesticated rather than educated. Starratt (2004), in reviewing a schooling situation driven by a scientific management approach, argues that schools have become sites of inauthentic learning. Bracey (2001) has argued that schools are being taken over by corporations that see human beings in terms of profit; thus, dollars signs are attached to students.

As a result, school leaders under the current high-stakes testing and scripted curricula are being reduced to overseers for a corporate capitalist schooling agenda that serves to produce better workers, not authentic human beings. The political climate that is driving education relies heavily on a scientific management approach to teaching, learning, and leading and poses an ethical dilemma for school leaders.

English (2008) and Sergiovanni (1999) describe the scenario succinctly when they argue that school leaders are in a box, faced with the dilemma of trying to be creative while simultaneously being saddled with bureaucratic mandates that impose on the lifeworld of schools. The dilemma is exacerbated by preparation programs for school leaders that are inundated with a managerial approach that makes too many leaders unconscious of the unethical practices that are cloaked under the language of leaving *no child left behind.*

 Preparation programs for school leaders are driven by a philosophical viewpoint that trains future school leaders to look primarily at the data, not the humanity of the school community. As a result, some school leaders may have unconsciously accepted an oppressor consciousness eloquently articulated by Freire (2000): "Because of their identification with the oppressor, they have no consciousness of themselves as persons or as members of an oppressed class" (p. 46). Schooled in administrator programs that have made them beings for others, some school leaders become tyrants.

Dantley (2005) cogently argues, "School leaders have been assigned to monitor pedagogical methods and curricula that convey these messages, which are often bathed in racist, sexist, and ageist language" (p. 40). Freire (2000) writes, "It is a rare peasant who, once 'promoted' to overseer, does not become more of a tyrant towards his former comrades than the owner himself" (p. 46). This may be particularly true for leaders who work in schools that are heavily populated with African American and Latino students and in environments where oppressive schooling conditions are allowed to reign.

Anyon's (1980) work on social class and the hidden curriculum of work could be applied to school leaders who serve working-class youth. Similar to the teachers that Anyon describes in working-class schools that use chalk and talk, some "school leaders attempt to implement scientific management or some other empirically based management system, without being cognizant of their social implications" (Dantley, 2005, p. 40). The transactional approach to leading schools leads to a *fake education* that the school community eventually sees as a process. The end goal becomes acquiescing to the process of domestication that is disguised as education.

Chomsky (2000) wrote, "The trilateral commission referred to schools as institutions responsible for the indoctrination of the young" (p. 17), and one has to wonder what role school leaders play in carrying out this unethical mandate. Foster (1986) posed similar questions:

1. How are society and culture reproduced through schooling?
2. Why are the sons and daughters of the underclass apt to be fathers and mothers of underclass children, too?
3. How is the culture of sexism and violence perpetuated?
4. Why can't schools break the cycle of class reproduction?

One of the ways to effectively ensure that school leaders acquiesce to unethical principles under the disguise of leaving no child left behind are the courses that school leaders take that do not offer critical discourse that would allow them to become conscious of these unethical principles. In an effort to raise test scores, school leaders become the face of oppression, forcing teachers to follow pacing guides and to throw useless knowledge at students.

Giroux (1991) contends, "Testing has also become the new ideological weapon in developing standardized curricula that ignore cultural diversity, in defining knowledge narrowly in terms of discrete skills and decontextualized bodies of information, and in ruthlessly expunging the language of ethics from the broader purpose of teaching and schooling" (p. x). Sergiovanni (1999) writes, "This test score emphasis puts enormous pressure on principals that becomes pressure on teachers that becomes pressure on students" (p. 83).

It then becomes apparent that Freire and Muhammad are correct when they declare one of the things that keep those in the ruling class in power is their ability to divide and conquer. Nowhere is this more evident than in schools where conflict between administrators and teachers, teachers and students, and students and students engulfs entire schools.

The problem confronting schools is beyond the *necessary illusions or manufactured crisis* that is centered on student outcomes. At the heart of the problem confronting educators is a moral and spiritual crisis. David Purpel and William McLaurin (2004) in their book *Reflections on the Moral and Spiritual Crisis in Education* have brought to the forefront the need to have a conversation that helps educators identify the meaning and purpose of their work.

Too often educators view their positions as merely a job, and sadly, it is one they have been conditioned to dislike. Often educators enter the profession with a theory Y perspective, meaning they are intrinsically motivated, but later, as they become engulfed with bureaucratic mandates, they shift to theory X where the prime motivating factor is a paycheck. What is needed to emancipate educators from the bureaucratic structure that have made them beings for others is the search for meaning.

The role of the educator is beyond the technical approaches that the organizers of the matrix have constructed. Educators should see their profession as being purposed and themselves likened unto the prophets of the past. These prophetic voices fought against unjust rulers and lifted the spirits of those who were subjugated by oppressive social structures. They were enlivened by visions that illuminated a newfound consciousness in their followers. Ultimately, they were seen as threats to those in power positions and were in many cases put to death. These prophets both past and present carved out new spaces for those deprived of justice, eventually altering the social structures that allowed those who suffered to see glimpses of the future.

More than ever, school leaders must address the moral and spiritual crises in education by not being fearful of naming and opposing mandates that come from on high. Freire (2000) eloquently describes what could happen when school leaders become conscious of the scientific management approach to education, or what he calls *banking*: "But sooner or later, these contradictions may lead formerly passive students [school leaders] to turn against their domestication and the attempt to domesticate reality. They may discover through existential experience that their present way of life is irreconcilable with their vocation to become fully human" (p. 75).

In addressing the moral and spiritual crises in education, school leaders will need to have a perfect love that casts out fear, making them challenge the unjust schooling conditions that ruin the lives of too many children. Dantley (2005) calls this type of leadership *purposive*: "Purposive leaders contend with the agenda of the hegemony while at the same time challenging those in the learning community to rise above the nihilistic predispositions that are pervasive throughout the community" (p. 41).

Purposive leadership challenges school leaders to become social justice activists that take action to solve problems such as unethical high-stakes testing, pacing guides, scripted teaching, and the racist undercurrent of education that is the engine behind the ongoing mis-education. The contributors in this book have argued for critical multicultural education, hopeful that such an approach could bring about equality of education for all students. Critical topics such as poverty, racism, sexual orientation, religious persecution, tracking, and numerous other issues that derail efforts to enhance education illuminate the necessity of a social justice approach to multicultural education for school leaders.

SOCIAL JUSTICE FOR SCHOOL LEADERS

What is social justice, and how does it work? Nieto and Bode (2012) offer a compelling definition of social justice as a "philosophy, an approach, and actions that embody treating all people with fairness, respect, dignity and generosity" (p. 11). They identify four assumptions that should undergird social justice education: (a) "challenging, confronting, disrupting misconceptions, untruths, and stereotypes that lead to structural inequality based on race, social class, gender, and other social and human differences" (p. 11); (b) "providing all students with sources necessary to learn to their full potential" (p. 12); (c) "drawing on the talents and strengths that students bring to their education" (p. 12); and (d) "creating a learning environment that promotes critical thinking and supports agency for social change" (p. 12).

Sleeter and Grant (2009) see social justice as a form of social reconstructionism that "deals more directly than the other approaches to oppression and social structural inequality based on race, social class, gender, and disability" (p. 198). The aforementioned descriptors of social justice as it relates to education demonstrate why school leaders are the key to addressing issues of social justice and ultimately to changing the direction of schools.

CONCLUSION

School leaders and prospective school leaders need to do a critical self-reflection on how they see themselves as leaders. Young and Laible (2000) cogently describe the necessity of reflection: "School leaders need to be continually aware and sensitive to the ways that more subtle forms of racism are conveyed in the educational process, through the dynamics of the school environment, and through individual practice" (p. 402). Engaging in a critical self-analysis will also require school leaders to engage in critical readings that can help them critique their practice.

Ultimately, school leaders must grow in historical knowledge, and as they grow in this knowledge they will be able to more clearly see the agenda of those who have historically shaped education to serve their interests. It is from these critical insights that school leaders who are truly concerned with touching the souls and changing the lives of their students will take action to transform the inequitable schooling conditions that too many children face. In this book, we have attempted to lay a critical foundation that would compel school leaders *to do good*.

REFLECTIVE STEPS FOR EDUCATIONAL LEADERS

1. Think culture first! As an educational leader, think about how you can develop a culture for learning.
2. Don't panic in the face of crisis by placing undue stress on teachers and students.
3. Move away from pacing guides and other processes that diminish teaching and learning.

4. Develop purposive leadership practices that will empower you to challenge the status quo.
5. Join and interact with a community of educational leaders who advocate for social justice.

DISCUSSION QUESTIONS

1. How might the focus on test scores impact an educational leader's leadership style?
2. What are your thoughts about the trilateral commission's view of schools as sites of indoctrination?
3. What are some ways educational leaders might play a role in perpetuating inequalities (race, social class, and gender)?
4. How do you see your role as an educational leader?
5. What are your thoughts about purposive leadership?
6. How would you incorporate social justice into your leadership practice?

REFERENCES

Anyon, J. (1980). Social class and the hidden curriculum of work. *Journal of Education* 162, no. 1: 67–92.
Bracey, G. (2001). *The war against America's public schools: Privatizing schools, commercializing education.* New York: Allyn & Bacon.
Chomsky, N. (2000). *Chomsky on mis-education.* Lanham, MD: Rowman & Littlefield.
Dantley, M. (2005). Moral leadership: Shaping the management paradigm. In F. English (Ed.), *The SAGE handbook of educational leadership: Advances in theory, research, and practice* (pp. 34–47). Thousand Oaks, CA: Sage.
Darder, A. (2002). *Reinventing Paulo Freire: A pedagogy of love.* Cambridge, MA: West View Press.
English, F. (2008). *The art of educational leadership.* Thousand Oaks, CA: Sage.
Foster, W. (1986). *Paradigms and promises: New approaches to educational administration.* New York: Prometheus Books.
Freire, P. (2000). *Pedagogy of the oppressed.* New York: Continuum.
Giroux, H. (1991). Series Foreword. In S. Maxcy (Ed.), *Educational leadership: A critical pragmatic perspective* (pp. ix–xv). New York: Bergin and Garvey.
Nieto, S., & P. Bode. (2012). *Affirming diversity: The sociopolitical context of multicultural education* (6th ed.). Boston, MA: Pearson.
Purpel, D., & W. McLaurin. (2004). *Reflections on the moral and spiritual crisis in education.* Santa Barbara: Bergin and Garvey.
Sergiovanni, T. (1999). *The lifeworld of leadership: Creating culture, community, and personal meaning in our schools.* San Francisco, CA: Jossey-Bass.
Sleeter, C., & C. Grant. (2009). *Making choice for multicultural education: Five approaches to race, class, and gender* (6th ed.). Hoboken, NJ: John Wiley & Sons.
Starratt, R. (2004). *Ethical leadership.* San Francisco, CA: Jossey-Bass.
Young, M., & J. Laible. (2000). White racism, antiracism, and school leadership preparation. *Journal of School Leadership* 10, no. 5: 374–415.

About the Editors

Abul Pitre is professor and department head of educational leadership and counseling at Prairie View A&M University, where he teaches multicultural education for educational leaders, and leadership. He was appointed Edinboro University's first named professor for his outstanding work in African American education and held the distinguished title of the Carter G. Woodson Professor of Education.

Dr. Tawannah G. Allen is an associate professor of educational leadership and graduate from The University of North Carolina at Chapel Hill. She has served as a district level administrator for human resources and curriculum and leadership in several North Carolina school districts. Her research agenda focuses on successful pathways to academic excellence for all children, especially African-American and Latino males.

Esrom Pitre is an assistant professor at the University of Houston-Clear Lake, where he teaches courses in educational leadership. Prior to working as an assistant professor at the University of Houston-Clear Lake, he was the principal of Donaldsonville High School. During his tenure as principal, he transformed the school to make it one of distinction.